I0481624

Adapted Leadership

Jacob Mullins

ISBN-10: 1724680269
ISBN-13: 978-1724680266

DEDICATION

This book is dedicated to Lavena. I've heard all the mother in law jokes. None of them applied to Lavena. She loved me like a son. We lost her to cancer when she was too young. Heaven received an angel on November 1, 2012. Thanks for teaching me what unconditional love looks like and raising an amazing woman that I get to call my wife.

CONTENTS

FORWARD

I became fascinated with leadership style early in my career. I'm not entirely sure why, but it was a subject that sparked a lot of curiosity in me as a young manager.

I spent over a decade studying leadership style. I read books, went to seminars, attended training, talked to mentors, and spent countless hours reading about it. Most of what I learned did not make sense. Some of it might have made sense in academia and concept, but it didn't seem to fit in the real world.

Leadership style has historically been broken down into rigid definitions. When identifying somebody's leadership style, you'd have to pick a style that most closely matched the individual. Many times in my career, I would see leaders that were so close to several styles that it was impossible to define their style. I also found it hard to define my own style.

To compound the issue, leadership style can be changed to maximize leadership potential. So let me get this straight. I need to change the style I can't define into another style while staying within it's rigid boundaries to be a great leader? It never felt right.

Adapted Leadership is a simple and practical book about leadership style. As you learn the concepts in this book, you'll find that leadership style is fluid and unique. You'll learn the attributes that shape style and how to use them to your advantage. You're getting years of proven leadership experience instead of classroom theory that hasn't been field-tested. You'll learn from my success and failure.

If you're looking for a long, boring book that will be difficult to understand, please toss this in the trash. If you want a book that's easy to follow and will profoundly improve your leadership potential, turn the page and let's rock!

SECTION 1
LAYING THE FOUNDATION

I am not afraid of an army of lions led
by a sheep; I am afraid of an army of
sheep led by a lion.

-Alexander the Great

1) WHAT IS LEADERSHIP?

I will never forget the day. It was cold and cloudy in mid December. The early signs of a long winter couldn't dampen my spirits. I was pumped.

I sat in the executive conference room of a very nice hotel. The faces around the table were all new to me. I sat across from my new boss. He was a very nice, yet imposing man standing well over 6 feet tall. All my new peers surrounded me around the large table. Standing at the front of the room was a consultant by the name of Dick Knox.

I had moved to New York about a month earlier. I was given my first big promotion to take over the dealer channel. I was going to be responsible for managing over 100 stores. This meeting was the first time we had assembled the leadership team for the New York market, and I was ready to shine.

The meeting had just started when Dick looked right at me. He asked me a simple question in front of everybody. "Jake, can you tell me the difference between management and leadership?" It was a brilliant, simple, and elegant question.

I sat there. No words were coming to my mouth.

My mind was racing to articulate an answer. The longer that question hung, the more desperate I became. *You idiot* I thought.

We sat in silence for about 15 seconds. It felt like a year. I was mortified. Here was this hotshot manager that just got moved to New York. I was young, but I had already built a national reputation in our company as a rising star. I sat with my new team unable to answer a basic question. Great way to make a first impression!

After witnessing my agony, Dick finally spoke up and ended the torture. He said this, "Management is getting things done through others. Leadership is inspiring others to accept your goals as their own."

Wow. This is one of those moments in my life that was burned so deeply into my brain that the memory has not faded over the last 15 years. This was partly due to my embarrassment, but it was mainly because of the impact that statement had on my career.

Dick tried to make me feel better by explaining that most executives couldn't answer that question correctly. Later in my career I would realize how right he was.

I had no idea at the time, but learning this basic tenant became the tipping point of my career and professional development. Leadership is so complicated, and yet can be so elegantly simple.

In order to understand leadership, it's vital to understand the difference between managing and leading. Let's start by breaking this down in its most simple form.

If you manage a team, you can make them do things because you have authority. You could tell your team to make sure that all their reports are done before leaving the office. They accept this task and do it because you, the manager, have the authority to utilize discipline, change compensation, or terminate employment. And so, reports are done.

Broken down it its simplest form, management is the practice of utilizing other people to complete tasks. These tasks can be repetitive and tactical, or the tasks could be broad and strategic.

Where does the leadership come in? Here's how I think about it. Leadership is something you demonstrate that increases your effectiveness as a manager. It's not an either/or relationship. You lead to aid management.

Let me put this into perspective for you. I was sitting in my office one day in Buffalo. This was two years after our infamous meeting. My boss walked in and closed the door. He never did that, so I knew it was serious.

"Jake, you're about to get a call that's going to change your life," his words dropped on the table like a bowling ball. He continued with his blunt tone, "A guy named Rudy is about to call you. He is going to offer you a promotion to go run the Arkansas market. Rudy is by far one of the most respected leaders in our company. Take it."

He shot up out of the chair across from my desk and briskly walked out of my office. Again, I was left speechless. Thankfully I learned how to talk later in my career!

Two minutes later, my phone rang. "Jake, this is Rudy," he said with a Caribbean accent. And then my life changed.

Rudy's leadership started with our first phone call. He had everything worked out with a job offer before he ever spoke to me. And I mean EVERYTHING. It's almost like he knew every question I would ask before they ever came out of my mouth.

Let me tell you what really impressed me. Rudy knew that I was about to marry the love of my life, Kelly. He knew her name and also knew that we were planning to get married in a month. He had already thought about supporting me since we were about to get married and deal with relocation at the same time. He knew so much about my life before we ever spoke. As the saying goes, he had me at hello. I gladly accepted the job.

I rushed home. Kelly saw that I was getting home early and met me at the front door. She could see that I was excited and had an eager look on her face. "We're moving to Arkansas!" I blurted out.

I didn't ask Kelly if this was okay, but I didn't have to. It was October, and she would do anything to avoid another Upstate New York winter. She started jumping up and down screaming. I think she was more excited than me! After about a minute she stopped screaming and then looked at me seriously and asked, "Wait, what's in Arkansas?"

Great question. I had no idea. Arkansas was a state that I had never considered visiting. Quite frankly, the only assumptions I had about Arkansas were negative. I also had no idea what my job would be like. All I knew was this. Rudy had engaged me so deeply in a 20 minute phone call that I was ready to uproot our life and move to Arkansas site unseen.

The next year was amazing. I learned so much from Rudy and the people I worked with. We dealt with a new competitor coming into our market and still grew our revenue. We went from being the lowest ranked market in the country to being number one.

Looking back, that year was the most influential of my career. I evolved from a manager with potential into a well-respected executive. It would take some time for me to fully appreciate what happened to me over that year.

I walked into the office one morning. It was a totally normal day. I think it was a Wednesday. Rudy called us into the conference room. Again, this was totally normal. As we all assembled around the table, he very softly said, "I've accepted a position as the VP/GM of Florida. Today is my last day here in the office."

There were a few people that burst out crying. It was devastating news. I felt like I had been gutted. I loved this guy. I always knew that my time with him would be limited, but dang. I wasn't ready. It happened so fast. It was like ripping a band-aid off!

Here's where the story gets interesting. As quickly as Rudy left, we had a new guy come in. The new guy was one of those managers that I'd like to forget. None of us were fans.

Over the next several months, our performance began to drop. We went from being the top market in the country back down to one of the lowest. Moral took a huge hit and things were not the same.

Maybe you've experienced something similar in your career. If you haven't, you're lucky. However, chances are very strong that you will experience something like this in your career, so be ready!

Here is where the contrast between managing and leading comes into play. When our new boss arrived, all of our duties stayed exactly the same. We had our staff meeting on the same day and time, we did the same reports, we kept the same distribution strategy, etc. I could go on and on about what stayed the same.

Think about it. What changed? I'll tell you. I changed. All my peers, direct reports, and support staff changed too. I didn't care anymore. When Rudy was there, I wanted to do anything and everything to support him. When he told me that he had a vision or a goal, it was immediately mine.

When I let Rudy down (and I did from time to time), it was awful. I felt so guilty. My head would hang in shame. You know when your Mom gives you that look? Yeah. That's how I felt. And yet, he NEVER got mad at me. Sometimes, he didn't even tell me that he was disappointed. He didn't have to. I was so bought in to his expectations, that I wanted it MORE than him.

I don't know what kind of image you have in your mind about Rudy. You are probably thinking that he was fun, engaging, caring, passionate, smart, and more. Yes, all those things were true. However, he was also tough as nails, set VERY high expectations for us, and cou d frustrate the living snot out of us.

The most important thing about Rudy is that he knew how to engage me at the deepest level. I always wanted to do right for him.

When the new guy came in, he did the opposite. He did things that made me lose respect for him. He wasn't likable and did not make any efforts to engage. As a result of his poor leadership, I didn't trust him.

At first, I rose to the occasion. I busted my tail and showed leadership to my team. I wasn't going to let the new guy ruin our progress. I was strong, and I was out in front of it.

As you may imagine, that didn't last long. After a few months, I just stopped trying as hard. I could not admit it at the time. I simply blamed him for all of our problems. As I matured and looked back on the situation years later, I was able to admit to myself that I lost interest, focus, discipline, and desire. I just shrugged my shoulders and said, "Screw it."

This is an extreme example. I went from one of my best bosses ever to one of the worst. However, think about the significance of this situation and how that relates to leadership and management.

Almost instantly, nothing changed and everything changed. My responsibilities were the same. My education was still there. I was still ambitious, shrewd, and quick. However, new guy affected my confidence, desire, happiness, and purpose. Because of this, I sucked.

After reading this, stop and take stock in your career. Do people do their jobs for you because you have authority? Or do those people do their jobs because they care so deeply about your goals that they make those goals their own?

Leadership is not about how people get things done. It's about *why* people get things done. And don't get me wrong; you need to be good at BOTH. I'll write another book on management!

In the following chapters, I'm going to help you understand how leadership works. I'll share the tenants that I have been so blessed to learn. I hope that after reading this book, leadership will make a little more sense to you.

After you learn how leadership works, I'm going to share the most important thing about leadership. Fluidity. It will make sense later, I promise. I wrote this book because most managers I've worked with over the years do not understand it. And when I say most, I mean MOST. I'm talking about brand new managers, seasoned executives getting ready to retire, and everything in between.

Don't feel bad. For a large chunk of my career, I didn't understand it either.

People may doubt what you say, but they will believe what you do.

-Lewis Cass

2) DO AS I DO, NOT AS I SAY

It was a chilly night. In fact, it was a little too chilly to be outside in a t-shirt. As the cool air drenched my skin, I didn't mind it. I was out of breath from peddling up a hill, and the cool air felt good.

I was fifteen years old. Since I wasn't old enough to drive yet, I had to ride my bike to work. I didn't mind riding a bike to work. Working for a paycheck when you're fifteen years old is a liberating experience. I would have walked if necessary.

I parked my bike out back where it was almost pitch black. I walked into the little Greek café about twenty minutes early for my shift. I was always early.

After walking in, I started my rounds of saying hi to everybody there. It wasn't time for the Saturday dinner rush yet, so everybody was calm.

I went into the back and sat down. I wanted to relax before my shift started. As I sat there, the owner came up to me. He never really showed any emotion. This day was no different.

"The other dishwasher called in sick tonight," he said flatly.

I had never washed dishes alone on a Saturday night, so I immediately got nervous. If it got busy like a normal

Saturday night, I might be able to keep up. However, I knew that I couldn't do it if the restaurant got any busier than normal.

I expressed my concern about keeping up, but I assured him that I would work my heart out.

"Can we use the cooking spray tonight so I don't get backed up on clay pots?" I felt like my request was fair since I was going solo for my first time.

Let me stop here and explain something. I enjoyed working there. The only issue I had with the job was the pot pies. The café was known for their pot pies. They were delicious. I bet half of the people that ate there ordered the darn things.

The problem with the pot pies is that they were baked in these little clay pots and served individually. The crust of the pot pie would stick to the rim of the clay pot and they were IMPOSSIBLE to scrub clean. It took forever to do them. I hated those stupid pots with a passion.

One day I asked a cook if he could spray a clay pot with non-stick cooking spray. He obliged. When the customer was done, the dish came back to me. I was amped with excitement to see the results of my experiment. I didn't need a rag, sponge, or scrub brush. The crust just fell off. Eek!

I went and talked to the owner about my discovery. Beaming with pride, I told him what happened. It would be so much easier to clean those things if we used cooking spray before making them!

"I'm not wasting money on cooking spray," he said flatly.

Dang. Talk about bursting my bubble! I didn't know much about business and management back then, but I didn't feel like his response was fair. I immediately felt like I didn't matter to him.

So there we stood. Short staffed for the night and I was worried about keeping up. Certainly we could use the cooking spray tonight.

"I told you last month that I'm not wasting money on that," he quipped with a little anger under his breath.

I got shot down again! I couldn't believe it.

Business was strong that night. As the rush started, I was hustling. Dishes were going out of the kitchen as fast as they came in. I was doing it!

After an hour of incredible pace, it got busier. In fact, I had never seen it this busy. Servers sounded stressed when they came back talking to the cooks. Everybody was moving fast and tempers were starting to show.

After about thirty minutes of this frenzy, dishes started piling up. They simply came at me faster than I could get them done. I was determined to keep up, but I just couldn't do it.

I heard a cook yelling at me, "Come on damn it, I need pots!"

Oh great, they were out of clay pots. I had a mountain of them stacked up waiting to be scrubbed.

"I'm working as fast as I can," I yelled back.

A few minutes later, the owner came back into the dish room. He started yelling at me because they were out of clay pots.

"It's our signature dish. Now move your ass and get me some clean pots!"

I was about ready to cry at this point. *Seriously?*

I looked at him and asked, "Can you please help me catch up?"

His facial expression said it all. With bewilderment on his face, he responded, "I own this place. I don't do dishes."

He walked back to his office and sat down. We were struggling to keep up, and he was sitting down. I was furious. How could he do this? How could he let me suffer alone without any help and then treat me like crap?

I stood there for a second. Then I did it. I took my apron off and shut down the dishwasher. I walked out the back door and was swallowed up by the darkness. I found my bike and rode home.

I didn't just quit; *I walked out and didn't say a word.* Looks like you're doing dishes now, jerk. That was the only job I ever walked out on. Months later, the place went out of business.

Part of being in management is accepting the fact that people will watch everything you do. They will observe your behavior at work and how you live your life outside the office. They see everything.

You can say a lot of great things, but it may not matter. People will hear your words, but they listen to your actions.

Your team will talk about you amongst each other no matter how much you try to avoid it. You may think you're boring, but people still talk. This may sound negative, but it can be harnessed for a good outcome. Let's explore.

Shortly after I started one of my first management jobs, I was out visiting my stores. I walked into one of my larger stores. It was only the second time that I had been there.

When I walked in, the store was slammed busy. There were customers everywhere. A waiting list had been established, and customers were getting frustrated with the wait time. At the sight of my entrance, the store manager got a sick look on her face.

She was worried that I was going to chastise her for not keeping up with the foot traffic. I happened to walk in when the store was overwhelmed and she didn't have a handle on the customer experience.

I greeted her with a chipper mood. "Let me drop my bag in the back. Then we can have some fun helping these customers!"

I rushed past her confused look and walked into the

back to drop my backpack. When I was back there, I thought about that Greek café. *Not me*, I thought.

I went out front and started helping. I did the most mundane tasks like answering the phones, filling up printers with paper, and taking some customer service calls. I filled in wherever I was needed. There was no job too trivial for me.

After the rush died down, I could get back to the business of managing. I needed to sit down with my store manager and go over some operational items.

When I asked her to come in the back so we could review those items, she seemed pretty happy. She was eager to return the favor and help me.

When we sat down in her office, she said, "I've never seen a district manager do that."

"Really?" I had a hard time believing that.

"No, really," she responded with confidence. "I've been doing this for years, and I've never seen a district manager roll up their sleeves like that. The team is already talking about it."

A light bulb went off. I immediately connected the dots between my experience in that café over 10 years ago and what just happened in one of my stores.

In order to be viewed as a leader, people need to know that you are willing to do whatever you ask them to do. You may not need to do it all the time, but they want to see that you would if necessary. Not only do people want to know that you are willing to do the work, they also want to know that you embody the values that the company expects from employees.

There is data to back this up. In 2013, Root Inc. did a study on management and leadership. In that study, it was found that only 26% of workers strongly agreed "that managers embody the values they expect from their employees." While that may seem low, there is direct, positive correlation to employee engagement, productivity, and turnover.

Everybody has experienced this thought. "If I were the manager, I would..." Fill in the blank. You've thought it a thousand times.

You won't be able to read everybody's mind on the small stuff. For example, if somebody thought you should have formatted a document differently, you wouldn't know unless they said something.

However, think about the big things. Embody the values of your company on and off the field. Think about that employee working in a crowded store or restaurant. If the store was slammed busy, what would they think?

If I was the manager, I would go in the back and hide. Of course not! You know exactly what they would think because you've thought it yourself. Be the manager you want managing you.

This also applies to your performance off the field. How many times have you seen this? Somebody you know and like gets promoted to management. Shortly after that promotion, your friend develops an ego. Their ego grows and you eventually see a different person. After some time, the friendship withers away.

Or how about this one? There is somebody that you respect in the office. Maybe you even look up to that person with sincere admiration. Then one day you find out that he or she is cheating on their spouse. Any feeling of professional admiration you once had is now gone because of their personal decisions.

Leadership starts here. You have to be a person that others want to be like - professionally and personally. And please, don't discount the personal side of this.

I once took over a team that was shell-shocked from a prior boss. The guy was really bad from what they told me. Naturally, this group was very hesitant around me as a new boss. I tried to break through, but the defenses were up. The team knew I had business acumen, but they were mostly concerned with my character. I took it slow and tried to gain their trust.

I was talking to one of the team members over coffee one morning. I told him that I was frustrated with my inability to engage the team. I asked him what I could do to gain everybody's trust.

"Our last boss was a really bad guy out of the office," he said. "We knew that it was only a matter of time until he screwed us over. His intentions were not good and he only cared about himself. We just want to know that you're a good person."

It was a bit of honesty that made perfect sense to me. I thanked him for the candor and started to think about it. How can I show this team the real Jake?

I do volunteer work in my spare time. I thought that I would ask if they wanted to do a team-building event by taking part in a volunteer event. They happily agreed to do it. The following week, we all painted a homeless shelter together. It was a humbling experience to serve. We had a great time together and got to see each other as good people willing to serve others.

The defenses dropped immediately. I had instant respect after that. I did not earn their respect because we did a volunteer project. I got the respect because they watched my every move while we were there. They wanted to see if I was simply putting on a show or if my servant heart was sincere. In a situation like this, you can't hide it. They saw my heart and extended trust without reservation.

Your team is watching your every move. People are going to talk about you no matter what. You may as well give them something good to talk about.

The best way to find yourself is through the service of others.

-Mahatma Ghandi

3) IT STARTS ON DAY ONE

As the chapter name indicates, leadership starts right away in any working relationship. However, this might take a little different direction than you thought. The primary subject we'll cover is caring. What? Caring? Yes, you read that correctly.

Let me explain. I'm going to start by asking you a question. Do you care about your people? I know what you're thinking. *Yes, of course I do. Why would he ask such a stupid question?*

I want to get something out of the way right now. Caring is not a feeling. It is not something in your heart. When it comes to leadership, caring is action. It is born in the heart, but it doesn't stop there.

Let's go back and unpack my first conversation with Rudy as an example. Before ever calling me, Rudy took to the time to research me. He talked to my prior boss several times. He looked at my past performance appraisals and talked to HR. He was also asking about my interests in life, hobbies, family, and more. He probably spent hours getting to know me before ever speaking a word to me.

When we had that first conversation, we spent about

90% of the time talking about me. It was after I hung up that I realized something. The remaining 10% of the conversation was Rudy asking me what I wanted to know about him as a person and a professional. *We didn't even talk about the job, expectations, or opportunities!*

If you think this sounds unusual, you would be correct. I have only seen this done a few times in my career. However, it was so impactful to me that I wrote about it my first book. Think about that.

In 2007, I was offered another promotion and asked to relocate to Florida. I was elated! Not only was this a great career opportunity, but Kelly and I had always dreamed of living in Florida. We quickly packed up and moved to Orlando.

At this point in my career, I was getting good. I felt like I could handle anything. I was confident in front of senior leadership, I was one of the top performers in our company, and I always beat budget. I was good, and I knew it.

When I started to assess my new role, I realized Florida had a major problem. Our market had the highest turnover in the country. Not only was it the highest, we were in a league of our own. The company average was about 30%. Our turnover was 95%.

This new reality hit me fast. In my first week on the job, I had about ten resignations submitted. Half of those resignations were managers. I looked at my team and had to accept that 95% of my people would quit over the next twelve months. OUCH!

This was a new challenge for me. I earned a degree in Business Administration and had over 10 years of management experience at this point. However, nobody ever taught me how to reduce turnover. I was puzzled.

Thank goodness I met Chris Mulligan, founder and CEO of TalentKeepers! As we were trying to figure out how to reduce our turnover, we discovered his company. They specialize in employee engagement and retention. As luck turns out, they were based in Orlando. It seemed like the good Lord was putting this all together, so we started working with TalentKeepers.

I learned so much from Chris and his team. They were great partners and mentors. I can't say enough good things about their company. One of the most impactful things they taught me is a practice called a Handshake Meeting. It's so brilliant and simple.

Imagine this. It's your first day on the job or your first day with a new boss. Your boss calls you into a private one on one meeting. In that meeting, your new boss discusses attributes that are most important to a working relationship with you. You talk about various competencies such as building trust, communication, performance recognition, and more.

During this discussion, your new boss is taking the time to ask how you feel about each of these attributes. She takes the time to ask about supervisors or coworkers that built strong trust with you in the past. How did they do it? What specifically made you trust them? How can we replicate that in this new working relationship?

After taking the time to walk through all these leadership and working relationship attributes, your new boss takes the time to recap everything you just talked about because she took copious notes. She also commits to working with you the way you prefer because now she understands what works for YOU.

Let's stop here. Wow!!! Think about it. Has any boss ever done this with you? If so, consider yourself lucky. Think about your current boss. What if your working relationship started like this on day one? More importantly, think about how different your working relationship would be today if he/she actually stuck to it and worked with you how they committed.

Now before we move on, the Handshake Meeting is

one component of a very effective platform. If your company has not utilized TalentKeepers to engage its workforce and reduce turnover, you should. Chris and his team taught me lessons that turbo-charged my career and exponentially increased my effectiveness as a leader.

So let's get back to Florida. When I first arrived and realized we had serious problems, I immediately engaged my direct report team. I knew they were the key. I did team building events, spent time getting to know them, asked about family, and focused my efforts on supporting them. My efforts were paying off. I could see them engaging me and stepping up their efforts.

By the time we had worked out contracts, planning, and all the other necessary components to launch TalentKeepers, I was several months into my new role. I had already built working relationships with my direct report team. I was working a LOT of hours and was deeply involved in the business. It was a chaotic transition, but I knew my team.

So let me be honest. We started the TalentKeepers implementation after I had been working with this team for several months. I was excited about the reporting insights and leadership development. However, I did not expect to get much out of the Handshake Meeting process. I thought some of my front line managers and new managers might get a ton of value out of it, but not me. After all, I was already engaging my direct report team on a deep level.

WRONG! Stupid me. I learned so much from my direct reports during those meetings. One of them told me that when she calls a boss to vent about something, she just wants to get things off her chest. After that, she likes a boss that takes a tough stance with her and tells her to suck it up. She doesn't want somebody to commiserate with her and tell her it's going to be okay. Well, guess what? I totally misread her and had been commiserating. Oops! I called myself out and we laughed about it.

Moving forward, I did it her way. When she started venting about an issue with a person or company policy, I just let her go until it felt like she had it all out. Then, I gave her a swift kick in the rear and told her to focus on what she could control. Get back out there and do something productive! She loved it. Of course, I couldn't do that with everybody.

In fact, let me share something interesting. I've been doing these Handshake Meetings with all my new direct reports for the past 10 years. I hear this comment a lot when I conduct them, "I didn't even know that about myself." When you take the time to verbalize topics that we don't often talk about, it gets you to really think about them.

Take feedback for instance. This topic is humorous to me. When you start talking about how somebody likes feedback, it always starts out the same. Most people will say, "Just give it to me straight. Hit me right between the eyes." WARNING. Dig into that one a little bit. Most people don't really mean it.

Karen, one of my direct reports in Florida, really surprised me. Let me introduce you to her. She was tough as nails. She was results oriented, straight to the point, blunt, driven, and smart. Karen always delivered feedback to her team very directly. Many times, it was too direct and I had to come back and help her understand that she ran over somebody too hard. As I describe her, I'm sure you know the type. You've worked with somebody like this before.

When I sat down with Karen to do her handshake meeting, she told me what I expected to hear. Even her explanation was blunt, "Just hit me. You know me Jake, don't f*** around. Just hit me between the eyes and that's how I get better." Typical Karen.

As we dug deeper into the conversation and we talked about some of her experiences, I started to notice something. She was describing some of the best coaches from her past and they all had something in common. Their feedback was encouraging and positive. As she continued talking about things, we both saw where this was going.

I will never forget this. After talking for while, Karen leaned back in her seat. She thought for a second and then said, "Well, damn Jake. I guess I like feedback sugar-coated." We both laughed hysterically. When we finished up our Handshake Meeting, she thanked me. She told me that she was grateful that I had taken the time (of course). However, she was extremely grateful because she learned a lot about herself. She also immediately recognized that she was delivering feedback to her direct reports without thinking about how they really wanted it.

After that one Handshake Meeting, I never had to go behind Karen and help her smooth out a situation again. She conducted her Handshake Meetings and adapted her feedback to each person's preference. It was amazing. One meeting. One conversation. Forever impacted.

Shannon was an assistant store manager at one of my largest stores in Florida. When I went in to visit that store, I was always impressed with her. She was so engaging with the employees, great with customers, and sharp as a tack.

I'm always looking for talent to put on the bench. I firmly believe that you should be looking for people to promote long before an opportunity becomes available. It helps you figure out strengths and areas of opportunity. You can create development plans that prepare future leaders so they hit the ground running on the first day after that big promotion.

I had a formal process for identifying future leaders. I would meet with my team to discuss our "bench" every month. We would agree on who should be on the list, development plans, and timeframes on when we think each person would be ready for the next step.

We conducted one of these meetings, and Shannon was not on the list. I asked her manager why we wouldn't identify Shannon as a future store manager. I thought she would rise above everybody and be our next promotion. The store manager told me that Shannon was not interested in a promotion for some reason. Hmm… I was curious.

I went and visited the store. I asked Shannon if we could talk. We sat down in private, and I asked about her career goals. She was very vague and couldn't articulate her long-term goals. I could sense that she knew, but I couldn't draw it out of her.

Let me stop here and explain something. If you want to care about an employee, you need to learn their dreams. Notice I did not say goals, I said dreams. Everybody has them, and it's never too late. Never. Once you understand what somebody really wants in life, you can figure out how to help them today.

You need to be ready. Sometimes you'll realize that the best way to support somebody's dream is to help them get hired into a different department. For example, you may have somebody that works for you in sales and he has a dream of becoming a Chief Marketing Officer. So guess what, you need to work diligently to help him get a job in your marketing department. This is not easy to do. Sometimes you'll have to do this for your best employees. Nobody wants to give away their star players to other departments, do they?

I sensed this was the case with Shannon. She didn't want to let me down by saying that her career path did not exist in my organization. I could see it on her face. I surprised her by talking openly about it. I told her that it was okay if she didn't want to stay in my organization. I would help her with anything. So I asked her, "Shannon, what's your dream in life?"

"I want to be a detective," her words poured out into

the room. I sat there in silence for a second. Didn't see that one coming! She explained that she had always dreamed of becoming a detective and that she had changed majors at school. She was majoring in law enforcement and was expected to graduate in less than a year.

Well then. No wonder she was coy about career planning. After she told me, I genuinely thanked her. I explained that it was better if we both knew about her dreams and the steps she was taking to make it a reality. I also committed that we would not bother her about becoming a store manager anymore.

I wasn't quite sure what to do for Shannon. She had a dream, and I wanted to help her achieve it. Of course I could support her school schedule. However, I thought that there had to be something else.

A few days later, I was reflecting on the meeting. For the first time in while, I was unsure how to help an employee support their long-term ambition. Then it hit me. Our company had an asset protection organization. Their primary responsibility was to investigate cases of theft, fraud, and other criminal activity. I also knew that they collaborated with law enforcement on a regular basis. That's it!

I called one of my good friends in asset protection. I explained the situation to him. I told him that I was not sure if Shannon would stay with our company long-term, but a job in asset protection would be a great learning experience as she worked towards her dream of becoming a detective. He loved the idea, but there were no jobs available at the time. He committed to let me know the minute something came up.

I was really excited. I went back to her store and asked Shannon for another meeting. I told her about my idea. I said that I have great relationships in asset protection and that I was going to do everything possible to get her hired into that organization. I didn't expect this, but she burst into tears. She was so overwhelmed with gratitude that she couldn't contain her joy. She was afraid that confiding in me would result in less commitment to her. She was afraid that we would see her as somebody with a foot out the door and withdraw.

For next six months, Shannon was absolutely my best superstar. She came up with ideas, always exceeded expectations, and had the best attitude. She really was one of the best. In fact, she saved my backside a few times.

I walked into my office early one morning. I'm one of those morning people, so it was like 6AM. I turned on my computer and there was an email from my friend in asset protection. The subject read, "Job Opening." I immediately called Shannon on her wireless phone. "Hello," she grumbled. *Oops, I woke her up.* I apologized for the early call. Then I told her, "Shannon, there is an asset protection job opening in Orlando." I could tell that she leapt out of bed. She started screaming in excitement.

I'm sure you've figured it out by now, she got the job. Let me tell you something honestly. It was hard to replace her. We took a performance hit when she left. You may think, was it worth it? The answer is simple. Yes.

She was good before I found out about her dreams. She was one of the greatest after I found out. I got six months of greatness. Plus, I would have lost her at some point anyway, right?

Helping Shannon also paid off in some other ways. It turns out, she was absolutely fabulous in asset protection. She helped me save millions of dollars in her role. She helped me uncover fraud issues that were so complex that we never would have uncovered them without her attention to detail. Again, she was a superstar.

About three years later, I was sitting in my office with the door closed. I was in budget planning hell. My eyes were crossed from looking at spreadsheets. My admin called me, "You have a visitor. She doesn't have an appointment, but she said you'll want to see her."

I wanted a break anyway. "Send her in," I said with curiosity in my voice.

In walks Shannon. I hadn't talked to her in quite a while, so I was pleasantly surprised. We hugged and exchanged pleasantries. She seemed really upbeat.

We sat down. She looked at me and started to get nervous. "I did it," she said. She explained that she was leaving the company. She just accepted a job as a detective. She also explained that she had me to thank for it. She explained that her position with asset protection allowed her to build relationships with local law enforcement. It also allowed her to prove her abilities and skip the traditional route of becoming a beat cop before getting promoted to detective.

This time, it was me that cried. I was so touched. Her hard work, education, and dedication allowed her to achieve the dream. I would never take credit for any of that. However, I was in a position to help construct a pathway. I invested a little time and energy to make that happen, and look at the results.

Turns out that I got more than six months of greatness in my organization. I accomplished something. I helped Shannon achieve her dream. In some ways, that feels better than achieving your own dream.

Caring is action. It starts in your heart, but is never completed until you take actions clearly demonstrating that your people are your priority.

We all see ourselves through our intentions, but we see others through their actions. Stop and think about that for a second. If you judge yourself in a situation, you have all the context of your experience and feelings leading up to that moment. If you judge somebody else's actions in a situation, you don't have any context.

It starts on day one. Every single time I get a new direct report, I conduct a Handshake Meeting first thing in the morning *on the first day.* I also take the time to get to know their dreams. When you do this right up front, it starts to lay the groundwork for becoming a great leader.

If somebody is going to care about your goals, you have to care about the individual employee's first. If you show them on day one that you care, they will return the favor when it counts.

True wisdom comes to each of us when we realize how little we understand about life, ourselves, and the world around us.

-Socrates

4) THE DUMBEST GUY IN THE ROOM

You've heard the expression. Surround yourself with good people. Makes sense, right? If you're going to be a successful manager, you need good people to carry out the work they are responsible to complete.

Let's take this a step further and talk about leadership. You have to do better than surrounding yourself with good people. You have to surround yourself with amazing people that are so talented that they humble you.

It was early in 2012. I just found out that I had been selected as the chief operating officer for a startup business. This wasn't just any startup. It was a startup owned by a very large, publicly traded company. I'm not going to disclose the company in an effort to keep attorney fees at bay. I'll say this, you would instantly recognize the company.

Overnight, I was catapulted into a massive role. It was like an out of body experience. Imagine playing baseball for a college one day, and then stepping up to Major League Baseball the next day. That's what it felt like to me. *Why was I chosen for this role?* So much responsibility was placed on my shoulders. Externally, I may have looked cool, collected, and ready for the challenge ahead.

Internally, I was nervous as hell!

We literally started this business with a big budget and a blank sheet of paper. We were entrusted by our parent company to figure out how to make it all work. So there I sat. I was responsible for so many functional areas of this new organization. Some of those functions were familiar to me. Others were as foreign as another language. In fact, I had to lead people in areas that I had no prior experience and no expertise.

I knew right away what had to be done. I needed to find the most talented people on the market. Believe me when I say this. Attracting talent is easy when you're in a startup backed by a huge, Fortune 100 company. So I did it. I assembled the Dream Team. I had a collection of professionals that were all at the top of their peer group.

The business was fast paced. No, it was light speed. We were all working flat out to commercially launch our business within 12 months of conception. Nobody thought it was possible except those of us that were doing it. It was electric. We moved mountains every day.

I came in one morning and got called into a meeting by one of my engineers. She told me that we had a problem. This was sort of a daily occurrence, so I didn't think anything of it. I walked into a conference room that was wrapped with whiteboard wallpaper (startups have whiteboard EVERYWHERE). There was scribble all over the walls, and I was surrounded by engineers that looked totally stressed.

I leisurely sipped my coffee and asked, "What's up guys? What's the problem de'jour?" One of my best engineers started to describe a technical issue to me. There was a problem with timing between two databases. As she was explaining it to me, several others started to chime in and talk about how the two databases were not exchanging information correctly through a middleware layer.

Okay, time to fess up. I didn't really understand most

of what they were talking about! It sounded like they were making half of this stuff up. Not only did I feel lost, but they were talking so fast and moving from one item to another without taking the time for me to understand. I started to feel dizzy.

I did understand something significant in the conversation. "We can't launch with this problem. It's a show stopper," said one of my engineers. Uh oh. I got that one. This was serious.

The technical banter went on for about 45 minutes. I honestly didn't understand a darn thing. I felt like an idiot. But wait, it gets better. After all this back and forth, one of my direct reports looks at me. She quipped, "Jake, what do you think we should do?"

Have you ever had one of those moments where you just wanted to crawl under a desk and make it all go away? I was having that moment. Immediately, all the noise stopped. It was so quiet you could hear a mouse fart! All eyes were fixed on me.

We had a massive problem. How do we fix it? Everybody wants to know and they asked *ME*! Of course I didn't have a clue. However, it gets better than that. *I didn't even understand the problem.* I was the dumbest guy in the room.

I took a deep breath and relaxed. After I felt myself start to focus, I came clean. "Guys, you're going to have to dumb it down for me," I admitted. I went into detail about what I did understand and what I didn't (which was pretty much all of it). I asked them to start from the beginning. I told them to explain it to me like I was clueless.

After dropping this little gem in the room, I was nervous about how they were going to respond. I expected them to think I was stupid. I expected them to think I was in over my head and didn't deserve my job. To be perfectly honest with you, I felt that way about 90% of the time.

What happened next might surprise you. Everybody in the room was excited to explain it to me. They were drawing on the white board walls, providing simple examples, and reveling in the fact that somebody was interested in their craft. Let's face it, explaining data collision caused by interface timing isn't exactly riveting subject matter.

Something else interesting happened in that meeting. Engineers started admitting to each other that they didn't fully understand what the other one was saying.

We spent a lot of time together that morning talking about the situation. The further we dug into it, the more we understood the problem and potential solutions. After hours of getting everybody on the same page, we had a plan. All I did was ask questions. My team came up with everything. Here's the awesome part. The plan worked and we launched.

Looking back on that situation, I realized something very important. I did not come up with any part of the solution. In fact, the team had to invest a few hours just to explain the problem to me. Even though I was the dumbest guy in the room, I was pivotal in finding the solution.

I had the courage to admit I was lost. That's hard to do when you're the boss. Most bosses struggle with this. When I admitted it, the precedence was set in the room. It was as if I told them, "It's okay if you don't understand something." After that was understood, more people started to open up about technical items they didn't understand. The candid dialogue enabled the discussion that ultimately led to our solution.

I was also worried that admitting my lack of knowledge on the subject would diminish my team's respect for me. I thought they would stop taking me seriously. However, the opposite happened. They respected me more. I set an example by being honest, candid, and letting people know that perfection is not required for success.

Surround yourself with greatness. Easy enough, right? Well, this is more complicated than it seems. The problem that most managers run into is the feeling of intimidation. How would you feel as a manager if you genuinely thought that all your direct reports were smarter and more talented than you? Be honest with yourself.

I'm going to be honest with you. For the better part of my career, I did not fully embrace this concept. I purposefully passed over very talented candidates at times. I thought some of them were so good that my bosses would think I was irrelevant. Some of them were so smart that they made me feel stupid. I deliberately passed them over. There, I admitted it.

There's a very good chance that you've done the same thing. When managers are honest with me, they always tell me that they've had similar feelings.

So what should you do? Simple, get over it right now. Remember the first chapter? Managers get things done through others. It wasn't until I started managing managers that I truly understood the importance of this concept. There are a lot of ways that you can evaluate a manager's performance. One of the most powerful measurements that I've used over the years is evaluating the level of talent a manager attracts and retains.

Let's take this one step deeper. You have to do more than surround yourself with talent. After hiring talented people, you need to enable them for success.

I was sitting in my office doing my normal email routine. My admin walks in with "that look" on her face. "Your expense report was rejected," she sighed as the words slowly escaped her mouth. She knew what was coming.

"Are you kidding me?" I was pissed. "What did I do this time? Did I forget to capitalize something?"

She told me that my boss wanted to know why I purchased three binders that cost a total of $18. I was responsible for a budget north of $100,000,000. My boss wanted to know why I spent a measly $18.

For context, I'll explain a couple things. This guy was a micro-manager to the extreme. And yes, he was a jerk. I'll be nice and keep his name out of the story. If you've ever worked for a micro-manager, you know my pain.

To accentuate the issue, I was absolutely the most organized person on the team. My game was tight. I followed every process to the letter. I was diligent about expenses – I spent every dollar like it was mine. I was under budget on expenses and over on revenue. I was a senior leader at this point in my career with an impeccable background.

Yet, I had to go justify an $18 expense. Let that marinate for a minute. I was incredibly organized, beating results every year, and experienced. I couldn't be trusted with an $18 decision? Come on! Empower me to do my thing!

This is an extreme example, I know. However, it's indicative of a much larger issue that I encounter on a regular basis. Let's examine a more subtle and insidious example of how this can manifest.

I had been entrusted to take over another market after my move to Florida. At this point in my career, I was well respected by my team, my peers, and senior leadership. I knew how to grow distribution like it was second nature.

I hired a very talented, young guy into a district manager position. He was very good, but he was still young and inexperienced. I was able to accelerate his distribution growth by helping out with commercial realtors, navigating company politics, and using all the shortcuts I had uncovered over the years.

Okay, hold on. I was doing it *for* him. I was so excited to show him the way and to make him successful. My heart was in the right place, but my actions were harmful. He needed to find his own way. After a while, I realized what I was doing. I stopped immediately and had a serious conversation with him. I apologized and committed that it would not happen again.

When you hire talented people, you have to unleash them. Let them show you *why* you hired them. If too much time is taken trying to control how they do things, motivation will evaporate like water on hot concrete.

Even though it may not seem like it, the end result of both of these examples was the same. That's a tough pill for me to swallow. How could I compare myself to a micro-managing jerk??

Here's the tough truth. If you look at a map, there are countless ways to get from one place to another. There is a fastest route, a shortest route, a route that maximizes highways, and a route that avoids highways. However, *all routes get you there.*

Not everybody will do things the way you do them. That's okay. Deal with it. Are you a micromanager? Here's the easiest way to tell. Do you find yourself saying things like *if I want something done right, I have to do it myself* or *I'm the only one that can do this*? If so, that's a good sign that you are micromanaging.

I need you to heed a powerful warning. If you micromanage people, they will do the very least amount of work to get by. Several studies have shown that micromanagement can be the worst morale killer in the workplace.

Sometimes empowerment is easy. In the case of my engineers, it was very easy. I couldn't do their work. I don't know how to write code. Empowerment came naturally to me in that situation because it was about survival.

What if it's something you're really good at yourself?

Ooh… Avoid the temptation, and let them do it. Step back and provide guidance when it's appropriate or requested. Remember, you hired excellence.

ADAPTED LEADERSHIP

If I won't be myself, then who will?

-Alfred Hitchcock

5) HEART-FELT HUMILITY

Right after I moved to Arkansas, Rudy told me about a store manager in Texas named Loyce. He had been doing some of his legendary research and thought she was ready for a promotion. He asked if I would consider her for a district manager position in Arkansas. I eagerly agreed to vet her out.

My first conversation with Loyce was hilarious. On the other end of the phone was this prominent Texas drawl. She was immediately engaging and had me laughing and smiling the entire time. She was also quick to tell me that she was a lot older than most of the people that work for her. "Everybody calls me Mama Loyce," she proudly boasted.

So, Mama Loyce it was! I loved her immediately. She was larger than life. After talking to her on the phone, I knew she had some very special people skills.

I have to stop here. I hope Loyce reads this book. If you do, please forgive me. I have to tell this story (she already knows which one)!!

Shortly after Loyce started working on my team, we scheduled a day to visit her stores together. We met at the office and got a game plan together for the day. After finished planning, we walked out to the parking lot. Loyce got all excited and shouted, "Oh, I got a new car! We have to take it!"

She had just bought a brand new Toyota Camry. It was fully loaded, and it was a hybrid. That was a huge deal because it was 2005. Hybrid cars were still rare at that time. In fact, it was the first one I had seen in person!

As we walked toward her shiny new car, she forcefully plopped her car keys in my hand. I looked at her confused. "I ain't driving," she said. "I hate it." So, I drove her new car all day.

I didn't realize this was indicative of a larger problem. See, Loyce *really* didn't like driving. She was easily distracted and got lost all the time. This was all compounded by the fact that she moved to a new state and that fancy new car didn't have GPS.

Late one night, my wife and I were sitting down to relax at home. We had just opened a bottle of wine. Life was good until my phone rang. I looked at the caller ID. It was Loyce. I was a bit surprised by the late call, so I snapped up the phone and quickly answered. On the other end was a very distraught Loyce. She was sobbing.

After a minute of her freaking out and me trying to calm her down, we started to communicate. "Dammit Jake, I'm lost," she cried. Okay, now we were getting somewhere. I'm a fixer, and I was confident that I could fix this.

"It's okay. Nothing to worry about Mama Loyce. I'll get you home," my voice was calm and reassuring. "Just tell me where you are, and I'll guide you home."

"Well crud, if I knew where I was, I wouldn't be lost now would I?"

Okay, that was a fair point. However, I was looking for something. *Anything.* She really had no idea. The more I asked, the more frustrated she became with the situation. So again, I'm a fixer. She told me that she was driving on a country road. So I asked her to tell me the next time she passed a state route sign so I could figure out what road she was on.

"There's a sign," she said while concentrating. "It says SR79. Does that sound familiar?"

State route 79? I thought. *What the hell?* I didn't even know where that was. So I told her to stay with me while I looked it up online (which meant MapQuest because this was before smartphones, remember). I pulled up the map of Arkansas on my computer and found 79. It ran from Memphis and went southwest through Arkansas down to Texas. The closest point to Little Rock was 45 miles away! I also didn't know how far she had gone.

I told her that I found 79. She was feeling relieved and I could hear it in her voice. I asked her to pay attention to the next intersection so she could tell me the cross street. She obliged and read off the next cross street about 30 seconds later.

I started to scan the map. Still scanning. Jeez. "Holy crap Loyce! How long have you been driving??" I figured out where she was. She had driven two hours in the wrong direction. She was about two and a half hours away from her house!!

I did what any respectable person (sucker) would do. I stayed on the phone with her for over 2 hours until she was close to home and knew where she was.

When she arrived at the office early the next morning, I walked to her office. "Come with me," my words were stern and I offered no explanation. Given the situation from the previous night, she didn't ask questions. We went to my car and I drove her to Best Buy. We walked in and I bought her the nicest GPS available.

Mama Loyce didn't put up a fight. She typically would never let somebody buy her something like that, but she knew that I wasn't messing around. I did not want a repeat of the previous night. I wasn't mad at her, I was worried. I really did care about her. I didn't want somebody on my team in that much distress.

I set the GPS up and showed her how to use it. She was very grateful and thanked me profusely.

If you think the story ends here, think again. Yeah... Loyce kept getting lost. First of all, she would get in arguments with the GPS. She would put in the destination and start on her way. A little while later the GPS would tell her to turn somewhere. She would think, *that's not right*. So she would go the opposite way or keep going straight.

It gets better. When the GPS would keep telling her to make a u-turn or go in the opposite direction, she would get pissed. She started "firing" the voices. She changed the default voice to the English accent guy. Well, she got mad at him and then changed it to the Aussie woman. Yep, she got pissed at her and changed it to the German guy. She went through every damn voice on the GPS and continued to get lost.

Loyce was a hot mess. She knew it too. If something was going to happen, it was going to happen to Loyce. There was always a story. There was always drama. It wasn't bad drama though, it was always hilarious. And when Loyce would tell you a story about something that happened to her, she was always laughing about it.

Her humility as a human was on full display for everybody to see. Thankfully, she came along in my life at a time when I really needed to learn humility.

When I met Loyce, it was at a turning point in my career. Up to that point, I had subscribed to a common saying, "Never let them see you sweat." I was proud to project an image of infallibility. I was well spoken and always aware of how people were reacting to me.

Let me reverse roles here for a second. If I had gotten lost like Loyce, I would not have called somebody from work, *especially* my boss. I would have called a friend or talked to strangers! I would have suffered in silence and showed up to work the next day like nothing ever happened.

In many respects, we were the same. We both had our

faults and quirks. We both cared deeply about our family, friends, and co-workers. We were both *very* good at our business. We understood store operations, process, and people management.

However, Loyce was very different than me. She had no problem putting her full character on display to people around her. Loyce was Loyce. What you saw is what you got. Everybody (and I mean everybody) had a Loyce story.

Let's be real about another difference between us. I was a good manager and leader when I met her. I improved the careers of others. However, Loyce *improved their lives*. It may sound melodramatic, but it's true.

Her team didn't care about her, they loved her. I had never witnessed a manager engage a team the way that she did. Starting on day one with caring? She had it nailed. She was Mama Loyce. She took care of everybody in her organization with such thoughtfulness.

Her humility taught me something vital about leadership. Up to that point, I had worked with people that were mostly like me. Everybody put their "best self" on display at work. We walked around like airbrushed images of ourselves. Hide the flaws and project something as close to perfection as possible.

Loyce didn't hide anything. You got the good, the bad, and the drive out into middle of nowhere Arkansas! Before working with Loyce, I thought that letting your team or boss see all your imperfections would be damaging.

I spent a lot of time observing Loyce and learning from her. Turns out, putting her entire self on display *made people respect her more*. Heck, it gave me more confidence in her as a direct report.

This makes sense if you step back and think about it. First of all, putting your humility on display makes you human. I'm sorry to be the person to break this to you. You're not perfect. We all have flaws and criticize ourselves constantly. It's a relief when you see that your boss or coworker is a real person.

You also know exactly where people stand. If I asked Loyce to do something and she didn't know how, she told me! She didn't try to pretend. She didn't run and ask somebody else. She would just put it right out in the open and ask for help.

Okay. Now think about this. When I asked her to do something that she was comfortable with, she would always get it done and exceed my expectations. Even if it was really hard, I knew she would do it. I had supreme confidence in her.

Have you ever given somebody a task or project when you weren't quite sure if they could do it? Yeah, it happens to me all the time. Not with Loyce. When she said she had it, she had it.

Here's another interesting thing about humility and human nature. If you put yours on display, others will reciprocate. The more I was around Loyce, the more I started to just put my whole self out there. The more I put myself on display with strengths and weaknesses, the more engaged people became around me.

Here's another benefit, and this one caught me by surprise. Putting your whole self out there reduces anxiety. I never considered myself "anxious." In fact, I felt like I was made of armor. I was cool under pressure. Nothing bothered me. Bring it on.

As I started to show more humility in the workplace, I felt different. There was this weight lifting from my shoulders. Pressure was blowing off like somebody cranked a valve wide open. After a while, something was missing. It was anxiety. Wait! Where the heck was that hiding all this time??

There's something else very important to consider. This is not creative license to be flawed to a point of being ineffective. You need to be good at your job and professional. Could you imagine your boss letting his guard down and telling you that he's got a problem with sexually harassing people in the office? Yikes!

I hope this is resonating with you. You may be thinking that it sounds great, but you're not quite sure how to do it. Simple, don't take yourself too seriously. Put that imperfect person out there for the world to see. We're all people.

Nearly all men can stand adversity, but if you want to test a man's character, give him power.

-Abraham Lincoln

6) WHO ARE YOU?

I want to take you back to Florida when I was dealing with my turnover issue. I was trying to get my head around this new market and the issues that plagued it. I was spending a lot of time in the field evaluating performance.

There was a store in Melbourne that was driving me nuts. I couldn't put my finger on it. The employees were not engaged at all. The morale seemed low. Something wasn't clicking.

The manager was responsive, but I didn't quite trust him. There were too many questions that danced across my mind. Just when I felt like he was doing okay, there would be something else that came up.

I got very frustrated with the situation. I usually didn't have any issues sniffing out problems and getting the truth to surface. It just wasn't working this time.

I surprised him with an unannounced store visit one day. When I showed up, he wasn't there. I approached one of the sales people, "Where's your manager?"

"Uh, he's at lunch," she stated nervously. I wasn't sure if she was nervous because I popped into the store unexpectedly or if it was my question.

I didn't think much of it. I started to help out with

the staff for a while. Everybody seemed on edge, so I grew more suspicious as time went by.

The manager strolled in about an hour later. He was trying to play it cool, but he was acting really nervous around me. Dang. Something was up. I just knew it.

After leaving the store that afternoon, I called my old friend in asset protection. "I have a hunch," I told him. "I think we have a manager that is taking advantage of us."

I explained everything to him and my theory about what was happening. I thought that maybe the manager was not coming to work all the time and his team was covering for him. It's the only thing I could come up with.

Over the next few weeks, we got really creative with technology. We came up with some ingenious ways to see if my hunch was right.

I was in my car one morning when the phone rang. "You sitting down?"

"I'm driving, so yes," I responded. "This must be good. Sounds like I may want to pull over!"

Our people in asset protection never had a flair for the dramatic. They saw fraud and abuse on a daily basis, so there wasn't much that got them excited. I could tell by the opening that something big was about to unfold.

"You were right," he said. "Well, kinda."

"What does that mean?" I was afraid to hear the answer.

"It's the entire store. All of them."

Huh? It took a while for him to explain, so here's the short version. The manager and assistant manager were only working about twenty hours a week. In turn, they were committing timecard fraud and allowing the hourly employees to do the same. They were all covering for each other!

I was smoking mad. I quickly engaged my human resource and legal partners to ensure we did things right. Within one week, I had fired every single employee in the store.

Who are you? You probably don't get asked that question a lot. Do you ever think about it though? It's a really important element to leadership. You probably think I'm talking about character. Well, I am. However, I want to take it a step further. Where does that character come from?

I ask this question a lot in business. What motivates you? I get a lot of answers that sound similar. You want to provide for your family. You want to set a good example for those you care about. You want to put your kids through college and retire.

Those answers are great and they are powerful motivators. However, I really want you to think about this. Go a level deeper.

Do you believe in God? If so, do you go to a church, synagogue, or mosque? What's the purpose of your life?

I'm going to share a few things about me. These are important things. I believe in God. I'm a Christian. Kelly, my wife, is a believer too. In fact, Christianity is a very important part of our lives. We are very active in our church along with our kids. We do a lot of volunteer work. We do bible study. We love our church family. Relax, I'm not Ned Flanders. I'm a pretty normal guy.

Why am I telling you this? It's really simple. I've been going to church for a long time. After all these years, I'm still learning new things about my faith and about me. Let me give you an example. I've probably heard about a thousand sermons that examined the book of Matthew. However, I still learn a little something new each time I hear our preacher reference it. I'm listening to different perspectives about the same writing.

As I continue to learn about God, I become a better person. Perfect? Absolutely not. But, every year I get better at extending grace and patience. I get better at unconditional love. I become wiser. I become stronger.

Is he telling me to go to church? No. I'm not telling you to do anything. However, I do expect you to ask some big questions of yourself. Why are you on this earth? Figure that out and infuse it into your professional life.

Ten years ago, my purpose in life was all over the place. I couldn't explain it with an elevator pitch, it was more like a blog post. If somebody asked me what my purpose in life was, they better get comfortable because it was a long-winded answer.

As I've pondered my life and spirit over the years, I've simplified things. My purpose now is very focused. Love others as God has loved us. Straight to the point (*and I can remember it now – important as you get older*).

I try to translate that into my career. It's not easy with politics, pressure, competition, and managers that lie to you about coming to work. In fact, I'm tested on a daily basis. Here's a recent example.

Last year I arrived at the office in a great mood. As you already know, I'm an early bird. I was the first one at work as normal. I had made a terrific cup of coffee and was feeling optimistic about the day. Then, I opened my email.

There was an email from somebody in our office. She had sent it to a client and copied me on it. In the message, she completely threw me under the bus. There was no advance warning. She did it intentionally in an effort to harm me. I was fuming.

Here is some context. This woman just didn't like me. I tried so many times to engage her. Despite my patience and efforts, nothing worked. She was just mean and nasty to me. She was one of those people that make other people look bad to feel better about herself. You know the type.

So there I sat. Delicious coffee was in my hand. I was ready to take on the world two minutes ago. Now, I was enraged. I wanted to lash out. I was already plotting out the things I was going to say to her. I planned on absolutely ripping into her. I was 100% in the right and she was going to pay for this crap. You can't treat people like that and get away it!

Stop. Breathe.

A gentle nudge from inside made me relax for a second. Would a reaction like that be inline with my purpose in life? No. Not at all.

But dang! I was so mad that the anger was getting the best of me. I knew what had to be done. I sat there in silence and prayed about it. I prayed for patience and grace. I prayed for wisdom and guidance.

Immediately, the anger was gone. I looked down at that delicious coffee and realized the day was mine. I was not going to let this situation ruin it for me. I was back to smiling and enjoying my morning.

So what did you do about the mean woman? Okay. Don't mistake my heart for weakness. I dealt with the situation. Just because I lead with my heart doesn't mean I'm weak. In fact, it's quite the opposite. I made it clear that I would not tolerate behavior like that from a peer. I just did it professionally and kept my cool the entire time.

Your purpose and spirit can also lift up others. During my tenure as a COO, I was having one of "those" days. Problems were bubbling up like a fizzy drink. I had an issue with a big contractor, and there was a lot of pressure on me to find a fix.

I got on a conference call. It was supposed to be one of those calls where nothing really happens so you can do "real" work in the background since nobody can see you. Come on, we've all been there.

About two minutes after dialing in, bang. Another big problem was discovered. Okay. Now I was paying attention. The discussion continued to escalate to the point where people arguing with each other. It was getting heated.

After hanging up, I had about enough of this day. I was beaten and battered. It was such a bad day that I just wanted to reset and try again tomorrow. I'm sure you can relate.

I got up and walked out of my office. I needed air. People were avoiding me and not looking in my direction. I'm sure that I had "the look" on my face. *Don't talk to Jake, he's about to explode.*

It was only about 1:30 in the afternoon. I felt like I needed a miracle to make it to the end of the day.

I walked into our break room to get something to drink. Since there was no whiskey, I had to settle for an iced tea. I sat there just trying to breathe before walking back to my office.

One of the women from our training team walked in. She was one of those people that always smiled, and always made you smile as a result. *Not now*, I thought. *I'm not in the mood for happy people!* Sound familiar?

She immediately started with the smiles and positive talk. Ugh. I had to talk and act like everything was okay. So, I did. I put on the "happy" face and started talking to her.

We talked about something funny that happened to her that morning. Her laugh was infectious and fun. Within five minutes, I was laughing hysterically with her.

About ten minutes after walking into that break room, I walked out and headed back to my office. I was happy again. My mood was positive, and I was ready to start dealing with issues one at a time. An entire day of crap was erased because of the interaction with one person.

I thought about that interaction for quite a while. I was humbled at the power of human interaction. She probably had no idea what she did for me, but I knew. As I thought about it, I realized that she did this all the time to everybody.

Think about your mood and attitude like a bank account. Each day, you start out with a balance. If we're honest with ourselves, we know that our balance is typically never the same. Sometimes, you dread the day and start off with a low balance. Other days, you're really excited about something and start off with a high balance.

Here is the important lesson about your attitude and how it affects leadership. Every person you come in contact with will either increase your balance or decrease it. It's really hard to interact with a person and walk away with the exact same balance.

So, think about that. Do you think you increase other people's balances? Do you improve their mood and attitude? Or do you make a withdrawal and leave people with less in the bank?

I'm going to level with you. I was not good at this early in my career. I was so ambitious that I really didn't think about it. You were either with me or you weren't. I was focused on the business and myself more than others.

Has anybody ever asked you this question? "Would you rather be respected or liked?" I've had hundreds of conversations like this over the years.

The answer is so simple. BOTH!!

Remember. Leadership is inspiring others to accept your goals as their own. Think back about your experience with people that were good leaders to you. Did you like or respect them? Both.

Be somebody that everybody else wants to be around. Be positive. Focus on making other people smile. Pay attention to how they react to you.

That day will come when you need something big. You'll need them to dig deep to make something happen. When the moment comes, they'll check your balance. "Oh, I see you have made several deposits here." Bingo.

A man must be big enough to admit his mistakes, smart enough to profit from them, and strong enough to correct them.

-John C. Maxwell

7) CELEBRATE MISTAKES

After working in Florida for a few years, I got moved into a new channel. My boss was really concerned about our dealer performance and asked me to take it over. Sales were declining, and there was not any new store growth.

He knew that the dealer channel was one of my strengths. I had done several big turnarounds with dealers around the country. He needed me, and I gladly accepted the challenge.

I settled into this new role quickly. Everything was familiar and comfortable. It was all the same challenges, barriers, and variables that I had encountered in the past. The only difference was geographic market. At least that's what I thought at the time.

I was supremely optimistic after a few weeks of evaluation. I saw no reason why we couldn't double our store count in a year. There were also some very poor performing dealers that I knew could be helped or leveraged into acquisition.

Unfortunately, things did not go as planned. In fact, it was a disaster. After about 3 months into the new job, I was drowning. Performance problems ran deep. It would take longer than expected to turn around our baseline operations. I was also forced to terminate some dealers for fraud. We lost about 30% of our stores due to these terminations. It had to be done and was right for our long-term success, but it created a lot of short-term pain.

Here was the kicker. My biggest strength was distribution growth. I could open new dealer stores like nobody else. It was my claim to fame in our company. How many stores had I opened up to this point? Zero.

Luckily, I had been courting one of our company's largest dealers to come to Florida. They had over 100 stores in other markets. We had worked on a plan for them to launch in Florida. We were targeting about 15-20 stores to open over the next 6 months. I developed an incentive plan for them that reduced their capital investment burden. This was going to be a nice kick-start to our store growth.

One of the owners called me unexpectedly one afternoon. I was sitting in my office. We got the pleasantries out of the way. Afterward, he quickly cut to the chase.

"I'm flying in tomorrow morning," he said. "I'd like to discuss some additional opportunities with you."

I thought this was a little strange. However, I didn't know the guy too well. I had never worked with him before. I had no idea what to expect, but I agreed to the meeting.

The next morning he arrived in our office. When he walked in, I was already prepared. I had reserved our boardroom. It was scattered with large real estate and construction drawings. I had several file folders piled up around the table with all the supporting documents. My computer screen was lit up with a planning spreadsheet.

I don't know why, but I had a bad feeling the minute he walked in. Something just felt wrong. It was like a dark cloud followed him in the room. He gave me no reason to feel like this. It was in my gut.

Again, we exchanged pleasantries quickly before

getting to it.

He started to explain his reason for the meeting with bold arrogance. "I've heard that you're struggling in this market to get stores opened," he said with a smirk. "Looks like I've got a lot of leverage here. I'm going to use it."

I didn't like where this was going. When he started this part of our conversation, his entire demeanor changed. He was smug and condescending. His eyes seemed to sink back into his head a little.

"I've put together a little proposal on how you're going to pay me," his words had slowed down. He was reaching into a folder and grabbed a sheet of paper. "This is the additional compensation I need in order for you to get your new stores."

He slid the paper across the table to me and leaned back in his chair. He had this posture like somebody that had just won a high-stakes game of chess. Check mate.

As I glanced at the paper, he continued. "You're going to pay it because you have no other option. I really don't care what you think of me. I didn't get wealthy passing up great opportunities like this."

I couldn't believe it. This son of a gun was trying to extort me. He was very well connected in our company. Somehow he found out that I was struggling. We were weeks away from opening his first store in Florida. He had the audacity to walk into my office and threaten me. He was demanding millions of dollars.

I'll provide a little more context. The incentive plan that I had already put in place for him was the most lucrative I had ever offered a dealer. He had a sweet heart deal to begin with, and then he tried to extort more.

This was the angriest I had ever been in a professional setting. We sat in silence for a few minutes while I digested it all. He was happily waiting for what he knew was coming. He won. He had me backed into a corner, and a big payday was coming.

I finally looked up. I stared him in the eyes. I'm a Scorpio. When I stare somebody down, it's unnerving. I stared at him for a few seconds with a steely face. The color started to drain from his face.

"No way," my words hit the room like a wrecking ball. I stood up and pointed at the door. "You just messed with the wrong guy. I don't do business like this. I never will."

Then it got even better! The guy threatened to call my regional president. He told me that they were good fishing buddies. He was confident that I would be fired.

The conversation escalated. It turned into a shouting match. It must have been bad because people had gathered outside the conference room to see what was going on.

I walked over to the doors and swung them open. He stormed out and pushed his way through the crowd of people that had assembled to investigate the commotion. He was cussing and yelling the entire way to the elevator.

After he rounded the corner, all eyes swung over to me. Their concerning eyes looked at me as if to say, "What just happened?"

I apologized for the commotion and assured everybody it was okay. I shared a few tidbits about the interaction and spent enough time with everybody to get a few laughs out of it. I needed them to know that things were fine and we all needed to get back to work. I knew it would be gossip all day, but I did what I could to squash it.

After I had a chance to calm down and process what just happened, I realized that my situation was bad. First of all, I knew this guy was tight with our regional president. I had no idea how he was going to react to what I just did. Maybe this was the end of my career. I didn't think that I would get fired. However, I could get blackballed for any promotions in the future. There were a lot of ways that a senior leader could make you miserable without firing you.

I also had the problem with my new store plan. I just

lost a major chunk of that plan and still hadn't opened any new stores. Not good.

I called an emergency meeting with my direct report team the next morning. I told them what happened the day before. They wanted all the juicy details, but I was ready to move on to solutions. He was out. What do we do now?

In that meeting, I admitted something to myself and to the team. I said a few things that have stuck with me. "Team, I'm failing you. I approached this dealer channel like I have so many times in my career. I'm doing something wrong. I need your help to figure this out."

The words fell out into the room before I even had a chance to think about what I was saying. That was not my style. I usually thought way ahead of what I said. After I said it, I observed the facial reactions in the room. Everybody looked confused at first.

As the team digested my words, I became more comfortable in saying it. I really was lost. I couldn't understand what the heck was going on. Why wasn't my plan working like it had so many times before?

I had no idea how long this emergency meeting would last. Turns out, it was an all-day meeting. After telling everybody that I was lost. We just started over. It began with brainstorming and we finished the day several hours later with a new strategic plan.

I want to explain what happened. This happened in 2009. Something changed. Our business was booming. However, there was an economic collapse in 2007 as you know. We were lucky. Our business was immune to it. At least that's what we thought.

As the economy struggled to rebound from such a massive hit, all our supporting industries and companies were impacted. This meant that some of the major components of our business such as real estate and finance had been radically changed. We needed to radically change some ways of doing business, but was hidden behind a cloak of strong revenue growth. Nobody saw it.

Now I'm getting to the heart of why I told this story. Thanks for sticking with me this long.

I sat down with my boss the next day. I had a lot to cover with him. I had thought about it all night and all morning. What was I going to say? Was he going to be mad? I really didn't know.

I thought a lot about what this meant for me. Sure, our results were lousy. However, the dealer channel was struggling before I got there. I found a bunch of fraud and cleaned it up. I stood up to a dealer that tried to extort money out of us. My team and I figured out some new ways to grow distribution. We figured out how the economy was impacting our business, and I knew our solution was going to be light years ahead of what the rest of the company was doing.

Time to fire up the excuse factory!! I don't want my boss thinking that I'm a slouch!

When I opened up the conversation, I surprised myself. I had been searching for the words all morning. I couldn't find them because I was looking in all the wrong places.

"I'm sorry," my words were soft. "I really let you down."

Whoa Jake! *What are you doing??* But the words were coming so fast and naturally that I couldn't stop them.

Rather than make excuses about a dirty dealer and external factors, I focused on my mistake. I should have seen it. I should have been asking those hard questions of myself when I started. It should not have taken me 3 months to figure out what had changed. The economic collapse in 2007 was serious, and I didn't factor it into my plan.

I wasn't quite sure how he would react, but I quickly found out. He was really cool about. He thanked me for being so honest with him and, most importantly, myself. He was confident that I was going to turn things around. He made me feel really good. A huge weight was lifted off my shoulders.

He also said that we needed to talk to our regional president about the situation right away. He was concerned that our performance was behind budget. He wanted to come clean early.

Our regional president was tough. Really tough. I had witnessed him melt faces off people in the past. He would unload on people in public meetings, and everybody was afraid of him. He expected results. He also happened to be fishing buddies with dirty dealer guy. Great.

"Let's figure out how to spin this in your favor," my boss said. He was immediately trying to protect me. I really appreciated what he was doing for me. It made me feel good that I just came clean with my boss and he was already formulating a plan to protect me. Then I did it again.

"I just want to tell him the truth," I said. "Just like I did with you. No BS." I was at a point where I didn't want to "spin" or "reposition" anything. As I told my boss, I should have seen this coming.

Turns out that my boss was really concerned about me doing this. He explained that he and I had a good relationship. However, doing this with our regional president would be career limiting. "If you do this, I can't protect you," he said.

Well then. You know what, I didn't want protecting. I should have done a better job. If I couldn't be honest, I didn't want to work there.

We scheduled the meeting. A few weeks later, my boss and I traveled to headquarters. I had put a slick presentation together that outlined my plan. I was prepared, but I was also ready to accept my fate.

It took a few hours. I fessed up to my mistakes without offering any excuses. I walked through my corrective action plan in detail. It was difficult because our regional president wasn't offering any reactions at all throughout the meeting. He asked a few questions along the way, but that's it. That was usually a very bad indication with him.

When I was done, he leaned back in his chair and folded his arms. Here it comes. The hammer blow. I sat down across from him and prepared for my beating. I knew it was coming. I felt exposed and weak in that moment. I had a fleeting feeling of remorse. Shoot. Maybe I shouldn't have done this.

He leaned forward. His arms still crossed. Now he was staring at me.

"That's the bravest thing I've ever seen somebody do at this company," his words were direct and powerful. "Don't get me wrong, your mistakes cost this company millions. You know it and I know it. But, thank you for owning it. I bet you'll never do that again, huh?"

I sat there stunned. Where was my beating? Where was his patented "hand slapping the table for dramatic effect" move?

He went on to share some of his own experiences along his career. He told me that he had made mistakes too. He told me about a few that dwarfed mine.

"Everybody makes mistakes," he said. "Hell, you're not trying hard enough if you don't make some mistakes. I get mad when people try to BS me about it."

I was genuinely shocked. I didn't expect this. In fact, being honest and apologizing for my mistake *accelerated* my career. He went on to explain that leaders like me were the future of our company, and I should be proud.

As we were leaving, he stopped me at the door. He shook my hand and held on to it. As he was still holding my hand, he pulled me close to him shared one more thing. "By the way, our mutual friend called me. He told me about your 'meeting' in Florida. He's a dirty, rotten scoundrel. Great job standing up to him." He gave my hand one last pump, and let go.

We all make mistakes. There is an art to making mistakes. If done right, this can elevate your leadership, character, and reputation.

The first rule in making mistakes is that you have to set some boundaries. These are not hard and fast rules, so it takes a lot of attention and common sense. So what do I mean by that?

What if somebody came into your office and told you that they just made a mistake like this? "I sexually harassed somebody down the hall. She ran out of the office crying." Or how about this? "I've been embezzling money, and I just put us out of business. I wanted you to be the first to know!"

There is a limit to what you can tolerate, and you have to be consistent. I tell people that I will not tolerate poor integrity or catastrophic mistakes. Everything else is negotiable.

This is where the art comes in. You'll need to be engaged in your business and constantly evaluating the position of your threshold.

I was working with a newly minted manager on a project in 2010. She was responsible for doing some store layout changes on a large scale. We were changing our plan-o-gram around to better mirror our customers' buying habits, and she was leading the design and implementation.

I asked her about the communication plan. When she shared it with me, I knew it wasn't going to work. She was way too dependent on email and didn't have a good follow up plan. I asked a bunch of questions and tried to get her think about all angles. She just wasn't getting it.

I let her keep going. As suspected, it did not go well. Our compliance was lower than 50%. She came into my office one day. She sat down and started to talk. About three sentences in, she started bawling. I gave her some tissues and assured her everything was okay. Once she calmed down, we started talking.

"I know exactly what I did," she said with steadfast determination. She explained it all to me. I was really impressed. She completely understood her mistake. She also came up with a plan on how she was going to roll it back out in a way that was effective.

In this case, I saw the problem coming. I could have easily stepped in and prevented it. However, what would she have learned? By allowing her to make a mistake, she learned a very valuable lesson that will stick with her for a lifetime. I also knew that if the rollout was botched, it wouldn't hurt our business results.

The second rule in making mistakes is to make them yourself. Your team actually wants to see you make mistakes. It makes them comfortable to replicate. By your actions, you let people know that it's okay to screw up.

There is a key though. You're already making mistakes whether you want to or not, and your team sees them. The difference is that you have to admit when it happens. You have to fess up and not make excuses.

Remember, I told my team in Florida that I was failing them and needed their help. I didn't make excuses. I was candid. After I did this, I immediately noticed a difference in their behavior. They all seemed more comfortable around me. The chemistry in our team was improved.

The last rule in making mistakes is to apologize. Your apologies should be genuine with a clear admittance that you were wrong. Don't try to package in some coaching or explanations. Just apologize and address anything else at a later time. An apology is a message that should stand-alone.

You also need to avoid weasel words. If you use them, it's not really an apology. Using a weasel word would sound something like this, "I'm sorry if *you took what I said wrong* and it offended you." Or maybe, "I'm sorry if what I did *might not have* been productive." Give me a break. I'm sure you've heard a politician give a non-apology apology like this before.

I was having a staff meeting one day and we were talking about a really challenging problem. There was a lot of brainstorming and debate going on.

After the meeting, one of my direct reports walked into my office. At this point in my career, I was openly asking for feedback and telling my team to let me know if they ever get upset with me.

She sat down and told me that I said something in the meeting that really bothered her. It was a completely innocuous statement. She took it wrong. Furthermore, she was getting feisty with some of the other team members in that meeting. I initially felt defensive. I thought that her behavior was worse than my completely innocent comment.

However, I realized that she had no idea what was in my heart. I said something that upset her, and she was brave enough to tell me. So, I did the right thing. I apologized. I told her that I should think about what I say before I say it. I asked for her forgiveness and told her that I would work hard to not let it happen again. I wasn't going through the motions either. I meant what I said.

She left happy. She was very happy in fact. I could have tried to explain it. I could have apologized and then coached her on her behavior in the meeting. I chose not to. If I would have done that, my apology would have been ineffective and forgotten in seconds.

Just remember this. If you say, "I'm sorry, but..." All that person hears is what comes after "but."

A body of men holding themselves accountable to nobody ought not be trusted by anybody.

-Thomas Paine

8) ACCOUNT ME IN

It was late in the afternoon. My heart was pounding as I walked toward the conference room. I was getting ready to conduct a meeting with my team, but my mind was still reeling from the meeting I just left.

He knew it was coming, but I had to let a district manager go. His performance was exceptional, but his behavior was unacceptable. He was a bully around the office. He had an ego that got in the way of teamwork, and nobody liked him.

I had spent months trying to coach him on it. I did everything I could to help him get perspective. Nothing worked. He was just a difficult person in his core. I put him on a performance improvement plan and made it clear that I would terminate him if things didn't improve.

He continued to push his luck. He obviously didn't believe that I would do it. I'm sure that several managers had given him empty threats in the past. I warned him that I wasn't that type of person.

I hate firing people even when they deserve it. If firing people ever gets easy, I'm going to get out of management. This one was no different. It was gut wrenching, but I did it. It was the right thing to do for our organization.

After I fired him, I walked into the conference room to address the team. My heart was still pounding. I was a little short of breath, but it was time to compose myself. I sat down and began the meeting.

"Team, I wanted to make you aware that John has left our business," my words were direct. "I know this probably comes as a shock to most of you. I wanted to get you guys together so I could make the announcement and let you know how we're going to manage the transition."

As I continued to talk, I could see that nobody was really paying attention to my words. Every jaw was on the floor. Nobody could hide their genuine shock.

I had only been managing this team for about three months. In that short amount of time, I fired the top performing district manager. I had been a little worried about how people were going to react, but then common sense kicked in.

When I watched this guy interact with the rest of my team, I thought about times when I had peers like this in the past. I had worked with a few bullies that were top performers. I couldn't stand them. All I had hoped was that my boss would fire them.

After I fired John, the others immediately leaned into me in a very positive way. They didn't do this because they were afraid of me. They did it because they respected me. They did it because they knew that people would be accountable in my organization.

Good employees want accountability in a team. Good people try hard and deliver results. They want to know that rules exist and that people will be held accountable for their actions. They want to win, and you win as a team.

Accountability is one of the easiest and hardest things to do as a leader. Accountability is also one of the biggest ways to drive performance and improvement from people.

Over the years, I've heard the term accountability used so much that it pushes me to the point of nausea sometimes. It's a word that is overused and often misunderstood.

Let's first start with the definition of accountability. Here is the Merriam Webster definition:

**Accountability: noun \ ə-ˌkaun-tə-ˈbi-lə-tē **
: the quality or state of being accountable; especially : an obligation or willingness to accept responsibility or to account for one's actions

Accountability is responsibility, plain and simple. Here's one of the biggest issues with responsibility in today's business environment. When people talk to me about accountability, 99% of the time they are talking about holding people responsible for bad behavior or poor results.

I want to address this right away. You hold people accountable for good things and bad things. And if you do it right, you should be spending about 80% or more of your time holding people accountable for the good things.

I started this chapter talking about holding somebody accountable for bad behavior. I did that on purpose because that's what most people think about when they think about accountability.

I want to step back and talk about the positive side of accountability. Think about it for a second. What does positive accountability sound like to you? Have you ever thought about it?

I want to share an example with you. This was the interaction that finally made it all click for me.

Let's go back to that distribution issue I had in Florida. After we figured out what our problems were and adjusted the plan, we started adding stores. We were growing like crazy. We went from abysmal performance to the number one market in the country.

I had somebody on my team that was new to our channel. I hired Denise away from our marketing team. She had never managed dealer stores before, but I knew she had tons of potential. She seemed like one of those people that I could put on any project and she would flourish.

Denise did not disappoint. She was awesome. Her market was growing like crazy because of her leadership. She quickly became a confidant, advisor, and close friend. She turned into my right hand.

We met with a dealer one day on a conference call. We were both sitting in my office with the dealer owner on the phone. I don't remember exactly what the issue was, but I remember that we were on the phone for about an hour and a half.

Denise's performance on the call was impressive. She handled herself very well. After the call was over, I hung up the phone and looked at Denise. "Great job," I said.

What happened next caught me by surprise. Denise looked at me with disappointment. I respected her a lot, so this bothered me tremendously. I thought to myself, *I just told you good job. What's wrong?*

I don't know why, but it just hit me. I realized that she wanted feedback. She was new to the dealer channel and didn't have the years of experience that I had. She knew she was doing well, but she wanted to know specifically *why* she was doing well.

I stopped. I turned around and looked at her and said, "I'm sorry Denise. I should be more specific. I really liked the way that you overcame his objections. That was perfect. You also had great reports prepared before we started. You had all the data ready and squashed every argument before it started..." I went on for several minutes.

Her entire demeanor changed. She went from

disappointed to very happy. It sparked some more conversation about her development and things we could work on in the coming months.

This is what positive accountability looks like. It clicked for me in that moment. If you find yourself saying "good job" to somebody, pause. Did you give them enough information?

I want to make something very clear to you. When it comes to positive accountability, you cannot give too much detail. When you notice somebody do something good, spend as much time as you can coaching the details. Talk about little things like tone of voice, body language, and collaboration efforts. Also, you want to provide the feedback immediately. This ensures that the situation is fresh in both of your minds.

This type of positive accountability is incredibly addictive. If you don't coach this way now, pay attention the next time you try it. The reaction from your direct report will solidify everything. Once somebody gets a taste of it, they want more.

A business that doesn't make money is a hobby. Results matter, always. There will always be expectations regarding behavior, strategy, actions, and results. If somebody cannot meet the minimum expectations for a role, there should be consequences.

Before we talk about holding others accountable for not meeting expectations, we need to talk about you. A leader has to be accountable for their own actions and behaviors before holding others accountable. That probably makes sense to you. However, managers are not going to fire themselves for not meeting expectations. So what does this look like in the real world?

First of all, let's talk about reciprocity. This may seem like common sense, but I see it done wrong all the time. I'm big on deadlines. I always try to tell people exactly when I want something done. I set the expectation that if you can't get something done on time, don't wait until the eleventh hour to tell me. Come to me early and let me know that you are having difficulty keeping up and you need a few more days. If fair, I will accommodate. If something prohibits a change in due date, I will help prioritize things for the employee and provide some additional help where needed.

Knowing this, I need to be accountable for getting things done on time myself. If I tell somebody that I will have an answer by tomorrow, I need to have it. If something prohibits me from getting it done, I need to let them know as early as possible and reset expectations.

It's a pretty simple concept. Do things the way that you expect them. It doesn't take a rocket scientist to figure out that this makes sense. However, I see this done incorrectly all the time. I see managers expect their team to deliver results that they cannot deliver themselves. I see managers expect their team to do activity at a level that they cannot do themselves. I see managers expect behavior that they are incapable of exhibiting themselves. I'm sure you have seen this yourself at some point.

As a manager, you will lose all credibility if you hold people accountable for standards different than yourself. Morale will take a huge hit, and you will experience low engagement that results in turnover and poor results.

Now, let's assume that you are holding yourself to high standards. Let's assume you are accountable for everything you expect from your team. How do you practice accountability when somebody on your team is not performing?

First, your expectations should be written down. This can be done in several ways. Expectations can be documented in annual appraisals, budgets, strategic plans, coaching, performance improvement plans, and more. If somebody is not performing to your expectations, first check to see if you have documented it at some point. Is it clear? Did your employee confirm understanding?

Next, you need to ensure that you are consistent all the time. You should expect the same results and activity from everybody. You should not water down the expectations for a particular person because they are struggling. That is not fair to the people that are delivering.

If somebody is not meeting expectations, don't move the goal line. For example, let's say that you tell somebody they will be placed on a performance improvement plan if they don't meet a target. They put in a lot of effort over the next few weeks, but fail to meet the target. Do you give them a second chance? That's a tough one. Once you start moving the goal line, where does it stop?

Practicing accountability in an organization is usually fun. If you are doing it right, 80% or more of your feedback will be positive. It's motivating to recognize winning behavior and results. However, accountability can also be one of the most gut wrenching things you do as a manager.

Let me tell you a little more about Denise. After she started to cut her teeth in the dealer channel, she had a manager reporting to her that was not meeting expectations. This guy had been with the company for over twenty years. He was a super nice guy with a great attitude. However, his results were not there.

When Denise and I started to talk about it, we both agreed that he had a lot of potential. We decided to set some really clear expectations and give him a lot of support. Denise started by spending a lot of time with him to figure out what he was missing. She quickly found several areas of opportunity that included things like organization, communication, and follow up. She coached him on these things and documented her expectations.

As time when on, he was missing a lot of the basic expectations that Denise had documented. He was forgetting to do reports, failing to communicate messages to his stores, and many other tactical items. They started to add up. The collective result of all this missed activity was poor business results.

Denise and I were discussing it one day in my office. "It's not working," she said. She was right. She was holding up her end of the bargain. She invested a lot of time to help him and had documented everything clearly for him.

After some discussion, we decided to put him on a performance improvement plan (PIP). I thought that it was time to deliver a wakeup call. I figured that if we put him on a PIP, he would realize that we were serious about our expectations. In over twenty years, he had never been placed on any form of discipline.

We got his attention. When Denise and I sat down to discuss the PIP with him, he was surprised. However, he did not push back. He quickly realized that Denise had been communicating clearly and it was his fault. He owned it and committed to do better.

I expected the story to end here. As I stated, he had a great attitude and was a long-term employee. I thoroughly expected him to step up and deliver. His attitude was awesome and he took responsibility for his actions. That is usually a formula for success.

However, the story continues. His performance did not improve. He started to execute most of the things that we laid out for him. His attitude was good and he was trying hard. He remained positive and committed to making the improvements we needed from him.

If you noticed, there was a key word in that last paragraph. He executed on *most* of the things we required. He did not execute *all* of them. Additionally, his performance was getting better, but it was not at the minimum level we expected.

Denise met with him every week to talk about progress on his PIP. I would join them a few times a month depending on my schedule. The communication remained constant so we could stay aligned.

After a few months, Denise and I were in my office discussing the situation. Although it made us both sick to our stomachs, we knew what had to be done.

"I hate to say it," she started. "We have to let him go. I've done everything to support his success, and it's just not working."

I looked out the window and pondered it for a second. "Yeah, you're right," my words were slow and deliberate.

We submitted all the documentation to HR. They supported the termination immediately. All the documentation and regular meetings showed HR that we had done everything to set him up for success. Even though he was a long-term employee, he had not done his part.

When the day came to terminate his employment, Denise and I agreed to do it together in my office. We were both torn up about it. This guy was so nice and had such a great attitude. I'd be lying if I said we didn't have second thoughts. We did, believe me.

When he walked into my office, he knew that he was getting terminated. He knew this was not another touch point meeting like we had been having over the past few months. He saw it coming a mile away.

Something very interesting happened in that meeting too. *He apologized to Denise for making her fire him.* That was a first for me!

It was an awful experience. I hated doing it, but we had to remain consistent. Denise's business benefitted from it. Her team's performance and morale continued to improve until she was one of the top performers in the country.

I wanted to share this experience with you for a couple reasons. First of all, this was one of those terminations that stands out to me as one of the hardest. As I mentioned earlier in the book, I hate firing people.

Sometimes, employees will make it easier on you by doing something really stupid. Even though I don't like firing people, sometimes I'm very happy when it's done because I just fired a terrible employee. However, this was one of those situations that was very hard. I didn't sleep for days afterward. I felt guilty. In my heart, I felt like maybe I could have done something else to make it work. In my mind, I knew that we did everything right and he just didn't do what we expected.

I also wanted to share this experience because this is exactly what accountability for missing expectations should look like. Denise did everything right. She set clear expectations and documented them. She ensured that he understood those expectations. She invested time to understand how she could support him. She coached him and documented the areas he was missing before implementing a formal PIP. When she wrote the PIP, it was clear and easy to execute. She held regular meetings with him to keep him updated on his progress. She didn't waiver.

This is the formula. If you have to hold somebody accountable not meeting expectations, you have to do it this way. This story ended in termination. However, I have way more stories that started out the same way and ended positively.

I had a store manager that got off track once. I had placed her on a PIP. Things were not going well, and I was starting to think about termination. She decided to take ownership at the eleventh hour and started to step up. She rapidly improved until she was our best store manager in the market. A few years later, I promoted her.

ADAPTED LEADERSHIP

SECTION 2
ADAPTED LEADERSHIP

He who has never learned to obey
cannot be a good commander.

-Aristotle

9) LEADERSHIP STYLES

I stood in front of the mirror. Frustration was setting in because I couldn't get the knot to look right on my tie. This wasn't just any tie either, this was my good luck tie! For guys, you know the one. It looks great on you and always complies into the perfect shape when you execute your favorite knot.

I finally got it. My tie looked good like it always did. My suit was crisp, and my face was clean-shaven. I took a breath and started to think. It was interview day, and I was feeling confident.

At 26 years old, I was not a seasoned manager. In fact, I barely knew what I was doing. I was young and inexperienced. However, I was starting to develop some leadership skills and felt ready for a bigger challenge.

I was interviewing for one of my first management jobs for a large, Fortune 500 company. I had done a fair amount of preparation before the interview because I really wanted the job. As I walked out my front door, I gave myself a pep talk. "You got this," I said out loud.

When I pulled in the parking lot, I was impressed with the 4 story building. It was draped in shiny, gold windows. I crossed through the lobby and looked around.

The place was imposing. It was endlessly lined with cubicles and bland artwork. I smelled cheap coffee and peppermint. I told the receptionist who I was, and she quickly led me into a small office. It was adorned with a few decorative accents and a no-frills, metal desk.

"Wait here, and she'll be in shortly," the receptionist said. I thanked her and took a seat.

At this point, I did what anybody else would do. I looked around. I was looking for some sort of explanation of who I was interviewing with and some hints about her interests. There were numerous pictures of a family in normal settings. I saw a picture of a couple high on a mountain. It looked like they were on some sort of snow ski vacation, but I couldn't be sure.

Before I could form any opinions, I heard somebody enter. She was tall, thin, and looked as if she was about 10 years older than me. She was dressed professionally, so I was relieved that I decided to wear a suit.

When we were exchanging pleasantries and beginning our conversation, I was forming a first impression of her. This woman seemed very mature, smart, and articulate. I started to feel intimidated.

I kept my cool and focused as we transitioned into the interview. She peppered me with questions. I'll never forget this interview because it was the first time somebody asked me questions that were deep and thought provoking. She was really probing me about management and people. I liked it because it gave me a chance to flex my intellectual muscles.

I was nailing the interview. It was going really good. She was like putty in my hands. She was professional, but she didn't have much of a poker face. She loved my answers. It was difficult to hide. I could tell she wanted me on her team. In fact, the longer the interview went on, the more confident I was feeling. This job was mine.

Then she hit me with a question that would change my life and career forever. "So, what's your leadership style?" Her question rolled off the tongue like an innocent inquiry.

My leader *style?* I sat there and thought about it. *What the hell is she asking me?* I had never been asked this question, nor had I ever thought about it.

I got really nervous. I froze like I had stepped into a deep freezer. I didn't understand what she wanted to know. Oh, crap! I started to panic as I tried to plot a way out of this situation.

Expectedly, I did what any other 26 year old would do in this situation. I started to lay down a steady stream of BS. Unfortunately, it wasn't even good BS.

Now let me stop here. Have you ever been in a situation where things get worse the more you talk? Yeah, I thought so. Well, this was my moment. It's like I couldn't put the shovel down. I just kept digging and digging. I don't remember exactly what I said, but I know it was total garbage.

Unfortunately, we ended the interview on that question. The last memory she had of me was terrible. It was me looking dazed and confused right before a giant wave of BS was vomited out of my mouth.

I walked out of that office and sat in my car. I almost started crying. I felt like an idiot. I blew it.

Miraculously, I got the job. When she called to make me an offer, I almost fell over. *Seriously, me? The guy who completely screwed up at the end of the interview?* I don't know why she picked me, but she did.

A few weeks later, I was in her office. We were talking about one of my stores. We had agreed on a plan of action and were about to wrap up. I couldn't help myself.

"In my interview, you asked me about my leadership style," my words were nervous and lacking confidence. "I don't think I answered that question very good. In fact, I know that I totally botched it. I thought it might help me if you explained your leadership style to me. So, what's your leadership style?"

The color immediately drained from her face. She looked as if she had just seen a ghost. She was terrified and nervous.

After a few seconds of contemplation, this woman started to lay down the most epic BS I had ever heard! In fact, I started to get concerned that I wasn't wearing boots! Her answer was so bad. She didn't have a clue how to respond and was embarrassed. So why did she ask me the question if she didn't understand it herself? I was perplexed.

I had no idea how important that moment was at the time. It ended up being the reason why I wrote this book.

Over the years, I've heard that question thousands of times. I've heard it from senior leaders, managers, direct reports, and clients. I never heard any good answers, so I started to get really curious about the topic. I started to read about leadership style and tried to figure mine out.

In 1939, a psychologist named Kurt Lewin led a group of researchers on a project. Their mission was to identify leadership styles and the effectiveness of each style. This was the first known publication on leadership style.

Lewin's study identified 3 styles of leadership. Those styles were authoritarian, democratic, and laissez-faire. Let's briefly explore how Lewin described each of these styles:

Authoritarian: This style is described as command and control. The leader gives very clear direction that includes what, how, and when. The leader draws a clear line between themself and the members of the team. Team members are rarely consulted for decisions.

Democratic: This style of leader provides guidance to team members instead of specific direction. This leader also participates with the members of the team. They seek input and guidance from their team before making decisions, but these leaders still retain the decision-making authority.

Laissez-Faire: These leaders offer no guidance to their team, or they offer very little guidance. Decisions are left to individuals on the team. Roles and responsibilities are often vague.

Since Lewin's work, there have been numerous publications about leadership style. I've read books, articles, academic papers, and attended seminars on leadership style.

Opinions about leadership style have evolved since Lewin's work. Today, most generally agree that there are more than three different leadership styles. However, there is disagreement on how many styles exist and the definition of those styles.

I've seen works that state there are seven different styles. I've seen some that identify twelve different styles. Why don't experts agree on this topic?

Before I get into teaching you about leadership style, I want to start with something very basic. Style. What is it? Let's look at Merriam Webster's definition of style:

**Style: noun \ ˈstī(-ə)l **

a : a distinctive manner of expression (as in writing or speech) writes with more attention to *style* than to content the flowery *style* of 18th century prose

b : a distinctive manner or custom of behaving or conducting oneself; the formal *style* of the court; his *style* is abrasive; also : a particular mode of living; in high *style*

c : a particular manner or technique by which something is done, created, or performed; a unique *style* of horseback riding; the classical *style* of dance

I like to use the last description used by Merriam Webster. Style is a particular manner or technique by which something is done.

Now let's go back to the beginning of the book. Leadership was defined as inspiring others to accept your goals as their own.

Let's tie these two things together and simplify the definition of leadership style. **Leadership style is the particular manner or technique used to inspire others to accept your goals as their own.**

Have you ever taken the time to really think about this? It took me years to get this. I was trying to figure it out before I had even defined leadership style. Once I did, I started to simplify the entire concept.

I don't believe that leadership style can be broken down into labels like most suggest. When I started to research the subject, I noticed a big problem.

If you search for leadership styles on the internet or in books, you'll find styles such as autocratic, democratic, laissez-faire, strategic, transformational, cross-cultural, facilitative, charismatic, and more (yes more).

As I studied these styles, I started to examine my boss very closely. As I read, I couldn't figure out which style she fit into. I read the various definitions, and I saw bits and pieces from each category that fit my boss.

I also started to think about my own leadership style. As I read various leadership style descriptions, I found the same problems evaluating myself. I found bits and pieces from each that described me. Furthermore, it felt like my style was different based on the situation.

You are unlike anybody else. You are unique. Just like me. So guess what, even if we were very similar, our styles would be a little different.

Your leadership style is determined by several attributes that can be dialed in with varying strengths. You can also utilize more than one attribute at a time. Let me introduce you to these attributes before I lose you.

Leadership Style Attributes

Direction		
Tell	----------------------------------	Ask
Decisions		
Unilateral	----------------------------------	Consult
Flexibility		
Rigid	----------------------------------	Open
Purpose		
Visionary	----------------------------------	Transactional
Change		
Innovate	----------------------------------	Preserve
Emotion		
Passion	----------------------------------	Subdued
Tone		
Forceful	----------------------------------	Positive
Motivation		
Internal	----------------------------------	External

Now, let's break each of these down and explain how they shape your style.

Direction

As a manager, you have authority over your subordinates. You can tell people to do things because you're the boss. You have the power to simply bark orders. You may think this is not effective, but you'd be wrong. There are times when telling somebody to do something is absolutely appropriate and effective.

Let's explore an extreme example. You're a soldier in battle. Your company is surrounded and the enemy is closing in. Death looks imminent. You're too young to die and scared as hell.

The commander comes running over to you. He starts shouting so you can hear him over the rapid gunfire, "Can you tell me how you feel about flanking to the right? I want to make sure you have a say in this."

Wait. What? That would be absurd! The best way to use authority in that situation is to deliver clear, deliberate orders.

You may not find yourself in a gun battle on foreign soil, but there will be times when you need to tell people what to do.

However, sometimes it's better to ask. Even if you know how to solve a problem, you may get more buy in if you ask. "How would you solve this problem?" Now it's their idea.

I'm going to clarify something. Asking may not be executed in the form of a question. Think about this. You may delegate a project to somebody on your team. You set some ground rules such as due date, what needs to be accomplished, etc. After setting those broad expectations, you let them figure out how to do it. Even without stating it as a question, you're asking them to figure it out.

Decisions

It's been a long day at work. You walk in the door mentally drained. You just want to change into something confortable and quickly distance yourself from the challenges you faced all day.

Your spouse walks in and cheerfully asks, "What do you want for dinner?"

OMG! I made like a thousand decisions today! You just don't have the mental stamina to make one more decision. We've all been there. You're not alone.

Managers make a lot of decisions. The bigger your job and responsibilities, the more decisions you have to make. At times, it can be the most exhausting thing about management.

Some decisions have to be made without consulting your direct reports. Disciplinary action is a great example. If you have to hold somebody accountable, you can't consult your team. You can't ask people to make the decision to fire themselves, right?

People love to be consulted when you make a decision, especially the big ones. Has your boss ever asked you for an opinion on a critical decision? How did you feel? You felt valued and trusted. You felt like you were a part of something bigger than your job.

Flexibility

Flexibility is one of those terms that can seduce. What could be wrong with being flexible? Shouldn't you always be flexible?

Yes. Flexibility is an incredible attribute to use at the right time. However, sometimes you need to be rigid like a board.

Let's look at the lowest hanging fruit. You are going to be bound by labor laws, regulation, and contracts. If you work for a public company, you'll be required to comply with the Sarbanes Oxley Act.

At times (okay, every day), you'll have employees challenge this. You'll hear comments like, "That's a complete waste of time." Or maybe you'll hear, "HQ has no idea what happens out here in the real world."

Leaders need to recognize when flexibility is not appropriate and stand tall. Explain why the process is important and that you are protecting your team and the company. After you've done your explaining, don't waiver.

On the flipside, you'll be asked to reconsider things that will not hurt if they are changed. Don't be a stubborn mule. If you can bend, then bend. This shows your team that you listen to feedback and take action on it.

Purpose

The purpose in any given situation may be different. If you want to grow revenue by 50% next year and completely transform your company, get ready. You'll need to be visionary.

Your team will want to hear where you see things going. You will have to tell a story about how you go from here to there. Each person will want to know how they fit into the story.

The process takes time. You're trying to help everybody else see the image that exists in your mind. The bigger the goal, the more complex the image. Be prepared to spend a lot of time on your vision if the goal is huge.

You might think, why wouldn't I want to be visionary *all the time*? Well, it's not practical. Let me give you an example.

Let's say that you wanted to roll out a new expense tracking process that was a bit more cumbersome. It's not a huge deal, but it's important to the administration of your team.

The purpose in this case is transactional. It's not grand. You don't need to invest a lot of time explaining the vision for an office with new, improved expense reports. "We're going to change the world, one expense report at a time."

It sounds silly and would be a waste of your time (and theirs). If you have laid a good foundation of leadership, you have credit in the bank. You have credit for things with transactional purpose when you need it.

Change

You are the captain of a ship. Something is wrong with the navigational plan. You are drifting off course in the wrong direction with a risk of being lost at sea.

Your team wants you to make a change. And please,

make it right now! Everybody's life depends on it! You make a change of course and announce it to the team. Everybody rejoices.

This is how it always works because *change is so easy*, right? Okay. We all know that's not true. In reality, change is tricky.

First of all, you have to consider people. Some people don't mind change at all. In fact, some people thrive on it. I happen to be one of those annoying "change people." I get bored. I like doing new things and trying new approaches.

However, some people think change is the worst thing that could happen. They need lots of attention when you introduce something new.

The second consideration with change is the environment or business condition. For example, you may be in a business environment that is doing very poorly. Like the ship drifting off course, the team wants change. They want to do something different so everybody's situation improves.

Be careful when things are going well. Change is much more difficult. People want to preserve tradition and do things that have always worked. This doesn't mean that you should avoid change, but be very thoughtful and strategic about what you plan to change. You should anticipate what the concerns will be and have a plan to address them before you announce anything.

Emotion

A leader needs to know when to show emotion and when to hide it. This is incredibly important to your style.

I had an employee that I challenged to hit a huge sales goal. I asked her to step up and hit a number she had never done before. Not even close.

When she waltzed into my office grinning ear to ear the following month, I knew what happened before she said a word. She told me that she hit the number. I jumped out of my chair screaming. She started screaming and jumping up and down.

She wanted me to react that way. What if I had looked at her and said, "Great job." Then, I immediately look back at my computer. How would she have felt? Yep, disappointed. Even though I praised her, she wanted emotion.

At this point, you're sensing a trend. It's not always best to show emotion. Sometimes you need to keep the emotion buried deep without an ounce of it seeping out.

When an employee comes in and tells you they messed something up, you're not happy. In fact, I've been through this many times. I've had some people fess up to mistakes that had me so pissed that I couldn't see straight.

So what do you do? Do you pound on the table? Do you start yelling? Do you show negative emotion that makes your employee feel terrible? No way. You hold that emotion in. Thank the employee for letting you know.

If necessary, tell them you need a little time to think and you'll discuss it later. Close the door and cuss up a storm. Call a friend and complain about the knucklehead on your team. Just whatever you do, don't display that emotion to your employee. You will cool off and be rational later, I promise. Bring that rational person to the next discussion.

Tone

Remember Dick Knox? He was the consultant that asked me about the difference between management and leadership.

Dick took me under his wing and mentored me for years. He spent a lot of time with me and he was an incredibly positive guy. I respected him immensely.

When Dick first started working with me, my

communication skills were poor. No, I didn't have an "area of opportunity." I sucked. However, I didn't know how bad it was.

Dick's coaching was not sinking in. Okay, think about it. One of the most important skills in communication is listening. See my issue?

He walked into my office one day and told me to sit down. However, he kept standing. His voice turned into steel, "Dammit Jake, you're an awful communicator. What's it going to take for you to understand?"

Whoa. I listened.

Your tone should be positive most of the time. You want to be somebody that others want to be around and work with. Negative people and negative tone have the reverse effect. Nobody wants to be a part of that.

However, sometimes you need to get serious because positive tone is not appropriate for the subject matter or situation. Sounding positive at the wrong time can also send a message of insincerity.

If you have to deliver bad news, just do it. Your team is mature enough to handle it. Get it done and out of the way and get back to positivity as quickly as possible.

Motivation

Motivation is not something static. When asked about it, most people give the big, broad answers that we discussed earlier in the book.

Motivation can also come in bite-sized chunks that come and go based on the situation. I used to play on a soccer team with some guys from work. It was just for fun. We would play a game and then drink beer while laughing about all the shenanigans. It was a total riot. We were not serious about competing at all.

We played a team one night that was getting pretty serious. We tried to calm them down and be cool. Come on, it's a beer league guys! Well, it didn't work. They played really dirty and were very aggressive.

I started to get mad. I wanted to beat these guys. Our entire team did, so we hustled hard that night. We played harder than any other night up to that point.

I was motivated by something temporary. I wasn't normally motivated to play that hard. Business is the same. Motivation will ebb and flow.

The important thing to understand about motivation is where it comes from.

If you wanted a promotion or pay increase, that motivation comes from within. You want it for you. Nobody is imposing that motivation on you.

Even though this motivation comes from within, a good leader can tap into that motivation and leverage it. A great leader can build somebody up and create internal motivation where it didn't exist before.

External motivation comes at you. If you were in a burning building, you would run to get out. You may not be a "runner" that loves doing 3 miles a day, but you run like the dickens to stay alive!

Business can impose external motivation on you. It could be something like sales being down year over year or a product quality issue. There are environmental and business conditions that create motivation.

Leaders can also impose motivation. If somebody is not performing on your team, you may need to step in. The motivation can come in the form of coaching or performance improvement plans.

You can also call in a favor. Don't underestimate the power of this. If you're a good leader, you've earned it. If somebody doesn't seem motivated to do something, tell them how important it is to you. Ask them to care about it because it means something to you.

Okay. I've filled your head with a bunch of attributes that will be difficult to remember 2 months after you've read this book. Okay, maybe you already forgot them. I understand.

Let me make this even more difficult before it gets easier, these attributes are not either-or relationships. Let's look at flexibility. On one extreme, you have "rigid." On the other end, you have "open." There are also a million shades between those extremes.

This is why it's hard to place somebody into a pre-labeled leadership style. It may be a pinch of one attribute and a heavy dose of another.

I've thrown a lot at you. I get it. However, I'm going to explain some common sense ways to remember these attributes in the coming chapters.

We'll look at some real world examples and how you can tweak these attributes to deliver the right style at the right time.

Be like water making its way through cracks. Do not be assertive, but adjust to the object and you shall find a way through it or around it. If nothing within you stays rigid, outward things will disclose themselves.

-Bruce Lee

10) FLUIDITY

Let's go back to Florida. In chapter two, I told you about the incredible turnover issue that met me when I arrived there.

Imagine trying to run a business where people were quitting faster than you could hire them. It caused so many problems. Everybody working there was miserable.

The first staff meeting I conducted with my district managers was pretty brutal. As I tried to calm things down and get people focused on some sort of structure, the meeting took on a life it's own. Comments were flying around the room and it was hard to keep track of who said what.

"You can't run a business like this. It's completely dysfunctional."

"What is headquarters going to do about this crap?"

"I don't know what to do. I think there are two managers in my district that are going to quit this week. I'll have to do their store audits and hire their replacements? Where will I find that kind of time?"

It was non-stop. I tried to reign the meeting in, but I clearly needed to let them blow off some steam. I also wanted to listen since I was new to the market and new to all of them.

After the meeting, I went into my office and sat in silence. I needed to think. I wasn't exactly sure how to solve this, but the situation was serious.

Given the dire circumstances, I knew what kind of leadership was needed. This team wanted a leader to make changes. The current situation wasn't working and everybody knew it. They wanted swift and decisive change.

They also wanted somebody to be visionary. Things were rough and they were miserable. They wanted somebody to tell them how things were going to improve. They wanted somebody to lay out a positive picture of the future so they could see light at the end of the tunnel.

I could also see that they were exhausted. They were looking for a leader to give them direction that was clear and strong. They were in battle and wanted somebody to lead them out of this mess. *Just tell me what to do.*

They also wanted passion. They needed it. A dire situation like this requires a lot of emotion to get people engaged.

I didn't know the operational strategy and tactics required to fix the situation yet. I still needed to figure that out. However, I understood how to leverage some of the leadership style attributes to get the team fully bought in to our mission. Visualized, my leadership style attributes looked something like this:

Direction		
Tell	[-]-------------------------------	Ask
Purpose		
Visionary	[-]-------------------------------	Transactional
Change		
Innovate	[-]-------------------------------	Preserve
Emotion		
Passion	[-]-------------------------------	Subdued

There was a knock at the door. I paused for second before answering, "Come in."

Standing in my door was Lori. She was one of my new district managers. I didn't know much about her, but I knew she had been a district manager in this market for a while. She was very well known and respected. At least I had one veteran.

"We need to talk," her voice was blunt as all her coffee, massive purse, and stylish accessories came plowing into my office.

I wasn't sure where this was going, but I definitely wanted to find out.

"It's worse than you think it is," her words were very matter of fact. "I know four managers that are quitting this week. They swore me to secrecy, so you can't tell them I said anything."

Good grief! I was flabbergasted. Four managers?

"How do you know?"

She laughed hysterically. "I know everything around here. Everybody talks to me, so I always know what's going on."

She was in my office for over an hour. We covered a lot of ground. Assuming I could trust everything she said, I felt way more informed after my conversation with her.

I also started to understand something very critical. Lori was different than the others. So I spent some time over the next couple weeks trying to understand her a little more.

First of all, Lori had been dragged through the mud. While district managers, store managers, and sales staff came and went, she remained. She put up with all the crap and remained a constant force. She was also more mature and experienced than the others.

She wanted visionary purpose and innovative change like the others. However, she did not want to be told what to do. She also wanted to be involved in every decision. Actually, she felt entitled to be included in all the big decisions. I don't blame her. I would have felt the same way.

I was at a point in my career when I started to practice the art of style fluidity.

I started with laying out a vision for everybody. I told them we were going to be the first market to truly understand turnover and how to proactively manage it. I gave some impassioned speeches about what it was going to be like for everybody after we figured it all out.

People in headquarters would be asking us how we did it. There would be career opportunities for everybody involved. Large bonuses would be paid out. They hung on every word and they all reacted very positively.

When I began working with TalentKeepers, that's when I started to adapt my leadership style attributes. I knew that Lori wanted to be included in everything. It was very important for her. In the same situation, my leadership attributes for Lori looked like this:

Direction		
Tell	----------------------[-]--------	Ask
Decisions		
Unilateral	-------------------------------[-]	Consult
Purpose		
Visionary	[-]-------------------------------	Transactional
Change		
Innovate	[-]-------------------------------	Preserve
Emotion		
Passion	[-]-------------------------------	Subdued

I called her one morning on my way into the office. I could always count on Lori as an early starter. After a little small talk, I told her that she was going to be my advisor on this rollout. She was going to be intimately involved determining how we roll this out and make it successful. She was thrilled.

I included her in all the planning meetings. While the

rest of my team did not want to be bothered, Lori wanted to be right in the middle of it. She was in her element. I asked her opinion a lot. I made the strategy hers just as much as it was mine.

It worked like a champ. The other district managers just wanted decisions made for them and to be told what direction we were going. However, Lori wanted to be involved in decisions and consulted on direction. My adapted style got everybody engaged.

It was the same problem. It was the same business condition. The only difference in this example was the people.

It was 5:30 PM and I was looking out my window at beautiful, sunny weather. My wife was at home waiting for me. I had a date with a cold beer, beautiful wife, and our pool. I was ready to pack it up for the night and get my summer on.

Our marketing director walked into my office. She looked pale and defeated. "You're not going to like this," she said with a soft voice.

I sighed. I glanced out the window for a second and then turned to her, "Can it wait until the morning?"

"No," her tone was sharp. "Headquarters is raising prices. It's bad. No, it's really f***ing bad."

So close. *I was almost out the door.* However, now my mind was focused on pricing.

"Let me see."

She passed a sheet of paper over to me. I reviewed it. As my eyes quickly raced over the pricing table, I felt my blood run cold.

"You've got to be kidding me. This can't be right."

She looked drained, "I didn't even want to show you. I knew you would lose your mind."

It was a right hook to the jaw. The company was having a tough quarter. Somebody in finance thought that we could fix it by putting the entire burden on the sales organization. I was willing to do my part, but dang.

Now my thoughts turned to the team. How do I roll this out? This is a tough one. How am I going to get them to accept tougher sales targets with higher prices as their own goal?

I was deliberate in my style attributes. The purpose of this change was transactional. We needed to make a pricing change because of margin pressure. There was no need to complicate it.

I also knew that my emotion had to be subdued. If I got all excited about our chance to accept higher pricing, nobody would have taken me seriously.

Even though my emotion was subdued, my tone was positive. I kept cool and expressed my confidence in them. We would get through this together.

I also didn't try to fool myself. The motivation was external for all of us. The company was having a tough year and imposed this on us.

Purpose		
Visionary	-------------------------[-]-----	Transactional
Emotion		
Passion	------------------------------[-]	Subdued
Tone		
Forceful	------------------------------[-]	Positive
Motivation		
Internal	----------------------[-]-------	External

I leaned into the external pressure. I explained everything about the company's current situation and the severity. I didn't leave anything out. My team completely understood the situation coming at them and it was motivating.

Our prices changed the following week. Sales immediately dropped. Our customer service lines lit up like a Christmas tree as customers called to complain about our new pricing. It was brutal.

Mike Tyson famously said, "Everybody has a plan until you get punched in the face." We got punched hard.

Nobody was ready for the severity of the drop or customer responses. Employees were complaining and I was quickly losing everybody.

This situation was evolving rapidly. I had managers and sales people that started giving up. They were acting defeated before we had a chance to really fight.

I realized that effort from my team was starting to evaporate, so I changed some of my style attributes. I used a more forceful tone when talking. I started giving clearer direction with more specifics. I needed to turn up the pressure. *Get in the game*!

Direction		
Tell	[-]------------------------------	Ask
Purpose		
Visionary	-------------------------[-]-----	Transactional
Emotion		
Passion	--[-]----------------------------	Subdued
Tone		
Forceful	----------[-]---------------------	Positive
Motivation		
Internal	-----------------------[-]-------	External

This helped convey a sense of urgency. At this point, I meant business. We had to focus on what we could control and forget about the rest. The only way to get my team on board was shift my tone and direction.

Our sales rebounded and we never looked back.

In this example, the people stayed the same. However, the situation changed and evolved.

The first section of this book covered the foundational elements required for leadership. If you can implement those concepts, congratulations! You are a good leader.

The key to being a *great* leader is the ability to identify the style needed for the moment. It requires you to rapidly adapt to constantly changing variables. You have to deliver the style necessary right this second. And be aware, it may change two minutes later.

If you notice the examples above, I'm not always thinking of all the style attributes. I think about the attributes that are relevant the situation. You can also see that I dial in the strength of each attribute like a volume knob. I ask myself how much is needed and apply accordingly. Remember, these are not like on and off switches. There are infinite shades of each attribute.

The reason I refer to this as fluidity is because that's what it feels like. When you start to deliberately practice adapted leadership, you will find your style flowing like a winding creek. You will weave in and around things smoothly, and nobody will notice.

At the heart of adapted leadership is situational awareness. I am arming you with some knowledge, but please prepare yourself. This is art. When you see somebody do this well, it's like watching a painter create a masterpiece.

Situational awareness requires clear understanding of three factors; environment, people, and self. You'll need to constantly evaluate these like a super computer crunching numbers. Let's explore.

Environment: This is the set of circumstances or conditions by which one is surrounded. Environment can be affected by countless things such as economy, culture, business conditions, product strategy, etc. I could go on and on. The important thing is to identify the circumstances that impact how your team feels.

For example, if you were on a team that was performing very well, people would feel good about the positive performance. The feeling of winning becomes a circumstance around the individual. This type of situation may cause resistance change because change can feel like a threat to success. There will be more resistance to unilateral decisions and rigidity as well.

People: Every person is different. Of course you know that. It's imperative that you know how each person wants you to act in a situation. You probably already knew that too.

Let me ask you a question. If an employee is harboring a feeling about something that effects their work, who's responsible for the lack of communication? If they were upset about something you did and didn't feel comfortable saying something to you, shame on them. Right? Well, no. It's always your responsibility to know where people stand.

That may sound like a tall order, but it's pretty easy. How do you do it? It's simple. Most people wear their emotions for the world to see. If you observe closely, body language and facial expressions should tell you.

But what if you can't tell? What if the employee has a good poker face and you are struggling to figure out how they feel? Just ask them.

Self: You are a major factor. No, I'm not really talking about your behavior. I'm talking about how people receive you. It will influence the style attributes that may need adjusting.

I had to make a difficult decision once and terminate an employee for poor performance. It's an awful, but necessary part of managing people sometimes. I found out afterward that one of my direct reports was best friends with the person I terminated. Oh boy. Have you been in this situation before?

For several months, she was not happy with me and very skeptical of what happened. Her friend was filling her mind with a bunch of biased opinions about me and what happened. Of course, I was the manager and couldn't discuss the specifics.

In this example, my sheer presence brought tension to

our interactions. It required me to dial in a more positive tone than normal. I had to do a little more asking instead of delivering direction. I included her in more decisions to build up some confidence.

You may also have something internal affecting the situation. Have you ever tried to be positive and uplifting after your day has been going terrible? It's pretty hard. You may risk sounding like you're not genuine.

All three factors can change rapidly or stay static for a long period of time. Just remember that it's your responsibility to constantly evaluate these factors. Once you understand where things stand, adjust those style attributes to match the condition.

ADAPTED LEADERSHIP

You don't have to swing hard to hit a
home run. If you got the timing, it'll go.

-Yogi Berra

11) RIGHT TIME, RIGHT PLACE

Let me take you back in time again for just a minute. It was a bitterly cold night in 2004, and I had agreed to take a guy I was mentoring out to dinner in Syracuse, NY. I walked into Dinosaur BBQ (all the Upstate NY people just started drooling), and the warm air was a relief when it hit me.

We sat down and ordered some beers. Jason was a bright guy. I enjoyed working with him. He worked at one of my dealer owned stores, so he wasn't technically in my chain of command. However, I managed the relationship with the owner of his company, so that's how we were connected.

As we drank our beers, I started asking him about some projects we had discussed a few months ago. He was a brand new manager, and he was a sponge that soaked up any new learning opportunity. I was helping him by selecting good leadership books, doing some coaching exercises with his team, and more.

We ate barbecue and had a great discussion. He was catching on quick. My gut told me this guy was going to be a good leader.

As we were getting ready to head out, he hit me with

107

a question. He asked, "When should I be a leader and when should I just be a manager?"

"Leadership is constant," I explained. "I think about leadership as something you layer on top of management. Leadership makes it easier to get things done through others."

The conversation went on for a little while longer, and then we left. I was back out in the bitter cold. I rushed to the car and started the engine. I was shivering while I waited for it to warm up.

As I sat there shivering, I thought about that last question again. I was satisfied that my answer was correct, but something was nagging at me. I thought that maybe he was asking a different question.

It was late in 2008. I was sitting in my office working on a budget exercise. I was deep in spreadsheets. My eyes were starting to cross, but I stuck with it.

At this point in my career, I was used to the budgeting process. It was a lot of time spent crunching numbers and going back and forth with HQ. This year was no different. I had to rework all my projections because of some new allocation assumptions. It's riveting stuff, I know.

I spent hours and hours working on it. It was so tedious, but it had to be done.

My office phone rang. It was my admin. She got straight to it, "I have Karen on the line. She said it's urgent."

Weird. She never called my office line.

"What the hell are you doing?" Her voice was ragged. I knew something was very wrong.

I responded, "What do you mean?"

"I've been trying to call and email you for almost an hour. All our systems are down!"

Oh no! I looked at my wireless phone. The battery

was dead. I must have plugged it in the night before, but not all the way. We've all done it, but that didn't make me feel any better. I felt awful.

She explained that we had a problem that took down all of our backend systems. We couldn't do anything for customers and it was an emergency situation.

We were in a critical situation that required leadership. However, I was sitting in my office working on spreadsheets.

It was an honest mistake. However, it was a mistake. I didn't have time to dwell on it. The situation needed immediate attention.

I scrambled a conference call for all my stores, IT, and all other support functions. I took the reigns.

A severe amount of external motivation was imposed on us. I adapted my style to match the situation. My tone was forceful. I showed a lot of passion in the call even though the purpose was transactional.

Direction		
Tell	----[-]---------------------------	Ask
Purpose		
Visionary	---------------------------------[-]	Transactional
Emotion		
Passion	[-]-------------------------------	Subdued
Tone		
Forceful	------[-]-------------------------	Positive
Motivation		
Internal	------------------------------[-]	External

Luckily, we got it fixed quickly and things returned to normal. Whew.

After the dust settled, I sat there. I have no idea why, but I thought back to that question that Jeremy asked me four years earlier. *When should I lead and when should I manage?* It clicked.

An hour earlier, I was being a manager. I was doing

tedious, administrative work. Now don't get me wrong, that was absolutely critical work. The process of budgeting is vital to any organization. You try to run a business without a budget. Good luck.

When I was working on that budget, I was not thinking about my team at all. My work was very process driven. I was paying attention to numbers and business variables.

All of the sudden, I got a call from Karen. In the blink of an eye, I had shifted to active leadership. My mind scrambled to determine the best way to get everybody to accept my goals and priorities as their own. I needed to transfer my sense of urgency to people that worked in my organization as well as support functions.

That's when I figured it out. Jason had asked me a question about managing versus leading. My answer to him was technically accurate. Leadership and management coexist. They happen simultaneously.

I think the question he was trying to ask should have been, "What's the difference between active and passive leadership?"

If you do some research, you'll find a bunch of different opinions about this topic. I like to keep things simple. Below is how I differentiate passive and active leadership.

Passive Leadership	Active Leadership
Actions and behaviors that happen naturally or habitually. These actions are occurring on a regular basis and **without conscious thought.**	Actions that occur as the **direct result of situational awareness**. Leadership style and behavior are thoughtfully evaluated before used.

I figured out the question and realized that leadership could be passive or active. Ah ha! That led me to think the next logical thought. *What's the answer to Jeremy's question?*

It took me a while to figure that one out. I spent a lot of time pondering that question over the next few years. Since I had never thought about it up to that point, I didn't really have a bunch of examples to learn from. I had to start thinking about it as I ran into different situations.

I'll start with passive leadership. Before we move on, I'd like to debunk something. I read some information about passive leadership in books and online. Maybe you've read some of the same articles. There are several opinions. The most common description of passive leadership is people that just let things happen to them. Translation: they are not leading.

I'm simple guy. That doesn't mean a darn bit of sense to me. It's an oxymoron. It's not a form of leadership if you are sitting back and letting things happen without guidance.

I've got a different take on this. Passive leadership is simply displaying leadership without thinking about it. It's right under the surface and just happens.

Most foundational elements of leadership will be passive. However, it's not exactly that simple. Before I confuse you, let me provide you some examples.

One of the first leadership foundations I shared with you in this book was setting an example for others. In management, people watch everything you do. They are watching you on and off the field. You should be setting a great example at all times.

I rarely think about it at this point in my career. In fact, I don't remember the last time I actively thought about setting a great example. I just do it without thinking.

Earlier in my career, however, this did not come naturally. I spent a lot of time thinking about how to set a great example. When a situation came up, I spent time assessing what was necessary from me to set the right example. If I didn't think about it, I was prone to make mistakes. I needed to mature as a person and learn through experience. After years of learning, the behaviors became automatic.

You'll probably spend a lot of time practicing active leadership on the foundational stuff early in your career. It will come more naturally as you mature and gain experience. That's perfectly okay and normal.

Does this mean that seasoned leaders don't practice active leadership on foundational elements? Well, that's not what I mean either.

Another foundational element we covered in the book is surrounding yourself with greatness. You need to surround yourself with people that humble you and are the best you can possibly find.

Again, this comes naturally to me. I don't even think about it. Much like the other foundational elements, I have learned how to do this over the years. However, I have encountered situations that have required very active leadership on this topic.

A few years ago, I had a very difficult situation come up. There was a severe economic problem in one of my markets. The competitive landscape changed dramatically and my business unit started to slip.

I did a situational analysis on my current environment. I needed different skill sets on my team, and I had to evaluate my organizational design. I couldn't do the same thing and expect different results.

My leadership was very active during this process. I was constantly thinking about people and skill sets during the hiring process. I thought about my own abilities and how to best augment my weaknesses. We needed people that were good at certain things that rounded us out as an organization.

After getting a new org design approved and some new team members hired, this became an area of passive leadership to me again.

Active leadership is the key to greatness. As I stated, you'll be active in foundational leadership early in your career. However, it's my goal to help you graduate to the next level.

The entire point of this book is learning how to adapt your style. You have to adapt your style at the right place and the right time. This can only be done actively. I don't care how good you get, you'll need to have situational awareness all the time. You will need to be thinking about environment, people, and yourself.

As we get into some tips on how to recognize those moments, let me give you an example to illustrate how timing is critical for adapted leadership style.

Let's assume that you are being forced to make a big change in your business. There is a new challenge that has forced the company to reorganize. Most people will understand that change is necessary to keep up, but there is one person on your team that you know has issues with change.

You roll out changes quickly. Your communication style is the same with everybody. You use the same direction, emotion, and tone with the entire team. All goes well since the need for change was apparent. However, there is one team member that is reacting very negatively to the entire situation. It's that person that doesn't like change. Oops, you forgot to consider how differently this team member would react to sweeping changes!

Direction		
Tell	[-]-----------------------------	Ask
Emotion		
Passion	-------------[-]-----------------	Subdued
Tone		
Forceful	----------[-]--------------------	Positive

Realizing the issue, you try to fix the issue by changing your emotion and tone with this individual after the changes have occurred. You adapt your leadership style and spend time talking to this person in an effort to "fix" the situation.

Direction		
Tell	----------------------[-]---------	Ask
Emotion		
Passion	--------------------------[-]----	Subdued
Tone		
Forceful	----------------------------[-]--	Positive

Despite your best efforts, nothing changes. The damage is done.

This is an example of the timing being off. Had your style been adapted prior to the rollout, you could have helped ease that person through a challenging transition.

Don't worry, you'll make this mistake at some point in your career. I've done it several times! It's not the end of the world, and you'll get through it. You simply missed an opportunity to used adapted leadership to get somebody that is adverse to change on board quickly. You lost productivity, you did not lose the war.

Here's the big question. How do you know *when* it's the right time to think about and adapt your style? Only you will be able to answer that question.

In an effort to help you identify those times, let's go back to the fundamental question. What is leadership style? Leadership style is the particular manner or technique used to inspire others to accept your goals as their own.

So the question you have to ask yourself is this? When should you be thinking about and actively adjusting your techniques to get others to accept your goals.

This is not an exact science. I really wish it were. If so, leadership would be a lot easier. Prepare yourself. This is art.

Here are some examples of situations that may demand active leadership:

- Getting a new direct report
- Taking over a new team
- Experiencing a change in business conditions
- Noticing a change in a team member
- A crisis emerges – internal or customer facing
- Business goals change
- A competitor makes a significant change

I wish there was an exact playbook that I could give you. However, there is nothing of the sort. You'll need to be on watch all the time.

The easiest way to identify when you'll need to lean in with active leadership is to remember the three elements of situational awareness. In the last chapter, we explored those three elements – environment, people, and self.

The easiest way to identify when you'll need to be actively leading is to constantly pay attention to these factors. Watch for new accomplishments, changes, and challenges. Be present in the moment and observe everything.

If you pay close attention, you'll know when it's time to drop everything and lead.

SECTION 3
PUTTING IT INTO PRACTICE

If you do not change direction, you may
end up where you are heading.

-Lao Tzu

12) OLD DOGS, NEW TRICKS

In chapter one, I opened this book about an experience I had with Dick Knox. I told you about the question he asked me and the impact it had on my career. He was the first person to get me thinking about the difference between management and leadership.

There is more to that story. Let me explain what I did not tell you about our experience with Knox Consulting.

We spent two days in that conference room. We covered a lot of ground. We all took DISC profile tests. We learned about personality types and how to better work together. We also learned about communication and how to build a strategic plan.

There was so much crammed into those two days. It was like a couple years of college got crammed into two days of learning. My head was spinning.

The first day that we all got back into the office, I'll never forget that feeling. I felt like I had learned so much. I was enlightened. However, I had this nagging thought. *Now what?*

I wasn't quite sure what to do with everything we learned. The only word I can use to describe that feeling is overwhelmed.

I grabbed a coffee and walked into the office of one of my peers. We were still getting to know one another since I was new. I wasn't quite sure how to broach the topic, so I waded in.

"So what did you think of that training?" My question was a bit timid.

"It was great," she responded.

I agreed and we had a little small talk about it. I finally got around to the point.

"I thought the training was awesome. However, I'm not sure where to start. It was overwhelming."

A wave of relief rushed over her face. Her response was quick, "Oh my gosh! I'm so glad you said that. Me too!"

Whew! I wasn't the only one. I made my rounds that morning talking to the others about the same thing. Turns out, we were all overwhelmed. At least I wasn't alone.

Later that morning, our boss called an impromptu meeting. He asked that we all rearrange our schedules and meet in the conference room in thirty minutes. We all followed orders.

We assembled in the conference room. All of us were there except the boss. We waited with some communal nervousness because we didn't know why the meeting was called.

He came strolling in with a big smile on his face. He was clearly in a great mood. He took his seat at the head of our conference table. He looked around at all of us.

"Team, I just wanted to thank you for the last couple days. It was great. I learned a lot and you all participated really well."

"It appears as if we've been doing it all wrong! In order to implement the things we learned, we all need to make some big changes. However, we learned so much that I'm not even sure where to start. I feel pretty overwhelmed."

Brutal honesty from the boss. I had no idea at the time, but this turned out to be a great learning lesson for me. I'm going to transfer that knowledge to you.

It turns out that Dick had this planned all along. He had been working with our boss before and after our training to help him with implementation. The strategy was brilliant.

During that initial meeting, we all agreed that we needed to make some changes. We created a plan on how we would implement incremental changes over time. We wrote those things down. We held each other accountable.

Over the next several months, things began to change. Even though I hadn't been there long, I could see the improvements. People worked together better. Our results were improving. We grew the business rapidly.

We executed on the incredible lessons that we learned. The training worked great. Even though we all felt overwhelmed after completing, we did it. *But why?*

At this point, I hope you're in a similar situation. I hope you've learned something or several things from this book.

So here's my question for you. Will you put those lessons into practice? *Will you change?*

I hope so. To increase the odds, I have a foolproof way to do it.

I also want to preface something. The longer you've been managing people, the more difficult this will be. That's why you have to trust me. Don't learn some lessons from me and then set this book down somewhere to collect dust. You're not finished yet.

Accepting change around you is much easier than changing yourself. Think about that for a second and let it sink in. I'm asking you to change how you think, react, behave, and lead. It's a tall order, I know.

Here's the secret. There is a time-tested method of implementing change within yourself. Here are the steps:

1. Be honest with yourself.
2. Write it down.
3. Commit to others.
4. Execute.
5. Seek feedback.

Now, let's explore each of these steps with some detail.

Be honest with yourself. What did you take away from this book? Go back and skim the chapters. I bet there are two categories of take away items. The first category is new information. You learned a few things (I hope). The second category is things you knew, but don't execute well. Be honest with yourself about what you want to do differently. Look yourself in the mirror and be real.

Write it down. Such a simple exercise, yet one of the most powerful. Write your goals down. What do you want to change after reading this? Maybe there are two things. Maybe there are two pages worth of stuff. Whatever it is, don't fool yourself by thinking you don't need to write it down. Every time Dick taught us a new concept, he would make us get our pens out. He would make us write down the phrase, "It is my responsibility to…" It helps you remember, and it automatically becomes a personal commitment. Keep your list in a secure place so you can refer back to it.

Commit to others. This is when accountability becomes real. Sit down with your team. Tell them you read a book and you've learned some things. Tell them you want to be a better leader. Go over your list with them. Tell them all the things you are going to change. Get ready, jaws will hit the floor. Believe me because I speak from experience.

However, they will help you execute on it. Who wouldn't want to be a part of helping their boss improve leadership skills.

Execute. This is the hardest part. Whether it's a new practice or changing a behavior, you'll be challenged to do something that doesn't come natural (yet). You'll run into a situation when instinct takes you in the wrong direction. You'll get a fleeting moment when you realize it. *Oh no, I'm not doing this right*. So, what happens? Do you have the courage to do it right? Prove it to yourself. And remember, your team is watching. You asked them to hold you accountable. Come on, you got this.

Seek feedback. After you start executing, how are you doing? Do you feel good about it? Are you seeing a change in your team? I hope you can answer all those questions positively. However, you may feel *really* good about it. Even if you do, you need feedback. Remember, you asked your team to keep you accountable. They expect you to ask for feedback. Some people may give it automatically, but most will not. It's intimidating to give constructive feedback to your boss. The feedback may confirm your actions. However, the feedback may have areas that require improvement. If so, go back to your list and write that feedback down. Make it real. Own it.

Over the years, I've been to countless training classes, read thousands of books, and worked with hundreds of mentors. Most of what I learned was complicated and difficult to execute.

When I learn something practical and useful, I want to implement it right away. Some of the books I read had concepts that were simple and easy, and I was so excited to utilize them. If I'm honest with you and myself, I've done this with varying success. In fact, I've had to go back and read books a second time because I didn't do anything with it after the first read. I put those books down convinced to implement new ideas. However, there have been times I completely failed to implement anything. In fact, I don't even remember all the book had to offer. So, I pick the book back up and read it again.

All those books, trainings, and lessons that I failed to implement had one thing in common. I didn't take the five steps outlined to implement change.

On the contrary, I was successful implementing change every single time I took those five steps. **Every. Single. Time.**

You're already a good leader. I know that because you took the time to read this book. If you can implement adapted leadership, you'll be one of the greats.

ADAPTED LEADERSHIP

Ask yourself what you want people to do for you, then grab the initiative and do it for them.

-Jesus Christ

13) LEAVE A LEGACY

I've had about twenty different managers since I got my first job. That's hard to believe! I hate to admit it, but I must be getting old.

As I reflected back on all my prior managers, I realized something. Only five of those managers were any good. The others were bad or ineffective.

Well, hold on because I'm not done. It gets worse. Only two of those managers were great. Only two! That's ten percent of the managers I've had in the past thirty years. Certainly my experience is not the norm! Or is it?

Gallup did two large-scale studies in 2012 that looked at employee engagement. In that study, they determined that about 70% of an employee's engagement is directly attributable to their supervisor. Makes sense if you think about it.

Here's the shocker. Gallup found that only 30% of employees in the US were engaged at work. That number was even worse when looking at the global figures. Only 13% of employees worldwide were engaged at work!

That's just frightening when you think about it. I had always thought that I just had bad luck with managers. I thought that other people probably had better experience with managers than me. Well, the data tells us that I'm not alone. We've got an epidemic of poor leadership in our country and around the world.

In fact, Officevibe did a large survey of the US workforce in 2017. In that survey, 75% of people said that their bad boss was the worst and most stressful part of their job! And to illustrate this point, 65% of all workers would rather have a new boss instead of a pay raise!

Let that sink in. We have information at our fingertips with all our modern technology. People are smarter than ever. Why in the world are we plagued by so much poor leadership?

The answer lies in how people are elevated into positions of management. Historically, people have been selected for positions of management based on prior job experience, knowledge, and success. In most cases, that prior experience does not involve managing others.

Let me give you an example. I have worked with many IT organizations over the years. Most of the managers and leaders of those organizations were educated in the field of information technology. They become good engineers first and then get selected to manage other engineers later in their tenure.

Is this model wrong? I don't think so. It happens this way for a reason. If you were educated as a medical doctor, are you fully equipped to manage an IT group? Probably not.

Here's where the model breaks down. When people get elevated into these positions of management, they are usually not equipped with the training necessary to lead people and their idiosyncrasies. I know I wasn't.

When I got my first management job, I was given an office and a phone. That's it. *Figure it out.* Okay.

I believe there is a brighter future. I believe we can do much better. Most importantly, I believe you can be a great leader.

Why is leadership so important? Obviously, great leadership helps us achieve our business goals. If we hit our goals, we make more money and open up more opportunities in the future.

Let's dig deeper though. Leadership is much more than just helping us achieve our business goals. The two great leaders that I referenced changed my life. Notice I didn't say career. I said *life* for a reason. I got better in and out of the office.

I urge you. Don't just manage people. Change their lives. Change the world. You have the ability to do it one person at a time.

Chances are very strong that you've had a bad boss. How miserable were you? It affected you at work and at home. It consumed your life.

Be a force for good. If you dedicate yourself to becoming a great leader, you will leave a legacy with those whom you lead. They will talk about you for years. When they apply the lessons you taught them, they will think about you and give thanks to your time together.

The most rewarding moments of my career have been helping others achieve their dreams. When you see the connection between the leadership you demonstrated and the actions that person took, it's better than money.

Let's review what it takes to be a great leader.

Lay the Foundation

What is Leadership? Management is getting things done through others. Leadership is inspiring others to accept your goals as their own. Know the difference and understand it deeply.

Do as I Do, Not as I Say. Your team will never want to do something you are not willing to do yourself. You have to prove it. People are watching you always. Set a good example for others to follow. Be somebody they aspire to be on and off the field.

It Starts on DAY ONE. You must care for your employees, and it needs to start immediately. Caring is action, not a feeling. Talk to your employees on the first day about their dreams. Use that as the basis for all your coaching in the future. Use your actions to demonstrate that you care on a regular basis.

The Dumbest Guy in the Room. Surround yourself with greatness. Find people that are so talented that they humble you. Enable them for success by unleashing them. They may not do things the way you do it, but you should empower them to find their own way. Your success will be measured in the level of talent you can attract on to your team. Let them lead you when necessary.

Heart-Felt Humility. You're not perfect, and nobody expects you to be perfect. Get comfortable with yourself. Be incredibly humble, and put your whole self out there for people to see. When you're seen as a person that's not perfect, people will respect you more.

Who are you? Figure out why you're on this earth. Have a big purpose in life. Channel that purpose into your daily activity. Be a person that constantly makes deposits into other people's happiness accounts. Focus on being respected and liked.

Celebrate Mistakes. If you're not making mistakes, you're not trying hard enough. Fail fast, and fail freely. Tell people you made mistakes. Own it without making excuses. Set an environment that is safe for your team to make mistakes. When they do, move on quickly.

Apply Adapted Leadership

After all the foundational elements of leadership are implemented, you are ready to advance. You are already a good leader. Heck, you may even be great by this point. Now let's kick it up a notch.

Leadership Style. Leadership style is the particular manner or technique used to inspire others to accept your goals as their own. Your leadership style is determined by several attributes that can be dialed in with varying strengths. You don't need to focus on all of them at the same time. You can focus on a few attributes that are relevant to the situation.

Direction		
Tell	-----------------------------------	Ask
Decisions		
Unilateral	-----------------------------------	Consult
Flexibility		
Rigid	-----------------------------------	Open
Purpose		
Visionary	-----------------------------------	Transactional
Change		
Innovate	-----------------------------------	Preserve
Emotion		
Passion	-----------------------------------	Subdued
Tone		
Forceful	-----------------------------------	Positive
Motivation		
Internal	-----------------------------------	External

Fluidity. Use situational awareness to gain a clear understanding of three factors; environment, people, and self. All three can change rapidly or stay static for a period of time. Remember that it's your responsibility to constantly evaluate. Once you understand where things stand, adjust the style attributes to match the condition.

Right Time, Right Place. What's the difference between active and passive leadership?

Passive Leadership	Active Leadership
Actions and behaviors that happen naturally or habitually. These actions are occurring on a regular basis and **without conscious thought.**	Actions that occur as the **direct result of situational awareness**. Leadership style and behavior are thoughtfully evaluated before used.

Active leadership is the key to greatness. You have to adapt your style at the right place and the right time. This can only be done actively. I don't care how good you get, you'll need to have situational awareness all the time. Here are some examples of situations that may demand active leadership:

- Getting a new direct report
- Taking over a new team
- Experiencing a change in business environment
- Noticing a change in a team member
- A crisis emerges – internal or customer facing
- Business goals change
- A competitor makes a significant change

Old Dogs, New Tricks. Here's my question for you. Will you put these lessons into practice? *Will you change?* There is a time-tested method of implementing change within yourself. Here are the steps:

1. Be honest with yourself.
2. Write it down.
3. Commit to others.

4. Execute.
5. Seek feedback.

Armed with this knowledge, you are unstoppable. Go out there and become a great leader. Your role is significant regardless of what you think.

I don't care if you are a CEO, mid-level executive, or a front line manager at a fast food restaurant. Your potential impact on other people's lives is exactly the same. I've seen managers become great leaders at every level. The people they lead are forever changed.

Think about all the things you wished people did for you in your life and your career. Go do those things for the people you work with. Don't build a reputation when you can leave a legacy.

ABOUT THE AUTHOR

Jacob Mullins is a proud husband and father of three beautiful children. They live on a farm south of Atlanta, GA. He has over 15 years of executive leadership experience for large, publicly traded companies. Jake is also the founder and CEO of ProLine Growth. ProLine Growth helps companies grow by providing strategic planning, employee engagement initiatives, sales acceleration, leadership training, and marketing strategy. Jake is available for training, keynote speaking, and facilitation of strategic planning meetings.

For more information, visit:
www.prolinegrowth.com

www.ingramcontent.com/pod-product-compliance
Lightning Source LLC
Chambersburg PA
CBHW051316220526
45468CB00004B/1371